KV-406-583

Education and Social Class

Edited by

Rick Rogers

GWENT COLLEGE OF HIGHER EDUCATION LIBRARY

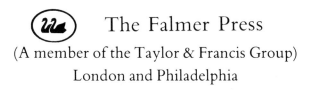

The Falmer Press

(A member of the Taylor & Francis Group)
London and Philadelphia

UK The Falmer Press, Falmer House, Barcombe, Lewes, East Sussex, BN8 5DL

USA The Falmer Press, Taylor & Francis Inc., 242 Cherry Street, Philadelphia, PA 19106-1906

Copyright © Selection and editorial material R. Rogers 1986

All rights reserved. No part of this publication may be reproduced, stored in a retrieval system, or transmitted in any form or by any means, electronic, mechanical, photocopying, recording or otherwise, without permission in writing from the Publisher.

First published 1986

120787

Library of Congress Cataloging in Publication Data

Main entry under title:

Education and social class.

 Papers from a conference organized by the Programme for Reform in Secondary Education (PRISE), held in Dec. 1983 at Homerton College, Cambridge.
 Bibliography: p.
 Includes indexes.
 1. Education—Social aspects—Great Britain—Congresses. 2. Social classes—Great Britain—Congresses. 3. Educational equalization—Great Britain—Congress. I. Rogers, Rick. II. Programme for Reform in Secondary Education (Great Britain).
LC191.8.G735 1986 85-20655
ISBN 1-85000-094-8
ISBN 1-85000-095-6 (pbk.)

Typeset in 11/13 Bembo by
Imago Publishing Ltd, Thame, Oxon

Printed in Great Britain by Taylor & Francis (Printers) Ltd, Basingstoke

Contents

Contents

Preface

In December 1983 the Programme for Reform in Secondary Education (PRISE) organized a conference at Homerton College, Cambridge, on *Education and Social Class*.

The papers in this collection were either prepared for the Conference, or submitted by the authors as contributions to discussion.

The introductory talk, giving an overview of the topic, was given by Dr Peter Mortimore, Director of ILEA Research and Statistics, and a co-author of *15,000 Hours* (the Rutter Report).

Most of the sessions of the Conference were spent in working groups, with those authors who were able to attend, discussing the themes under the headings:

(i)   curriculum;
(ii) examinations;
(iii) privatization, and the sociology of the school;
(iv) race and language;
(v) work;
(vi) gender.

An edited summary of these discussions follows the relevant papers, as a commentary on the issues. All six topics have been reverberating through the educational debates of the last ten years or more. For some reason discussion of their connection with social class has been strangely muted.

The Conference gave ample evidence that PRISE was right to bring into the open the fact that social class in Britain still exerts considerable impact on the life chances, and life styles of young people.

The change to comprehensive schools has scarcely dented the deep social divisions in our society, partly because the reorganized schools have largely failed so far to construct a comprehensive *curriculum* which would make a reality of equal opportunity and equal value. This is a thread which runs through many of the discussions.

There is considerable ferment, at both theoretical and practical levels, about secondary education in particular, in terms of the curriculum, a changing examination system, and the tension between academic and vocational emphases. With increasing intervention, both from central and local government, there is no doubt that the next five years or so will be vital in giving shape to a framework on which schools can build something firm and coherent for the coming generation.

The papers and comments in this collection raise most of the fundamental questions, and go some way to indicating possible directions for change and development. Unless teachers, and all those with a concern for education, work together to resolve the complex challenges, the rift between the two nations referred to by contributors will continue to widen.

Education and Social Class

Peter Mortimore and Jo Mortimore

Introduction

The state education system of England and Wales, like those of many
other societies, faces a number of difficulties: a shrinking population
has coincided with an economic recession; youth unemployment is
causing many pupils·to question the value of schooling; complex
problems concerning the effects of institutionalized racism and sexism
have been identified; and, because some parts of the media choose to
attack constantly the work of teachers, public confidence in the system
sometimes appears lacking. In addition, those who work as headteachers or as officers in local education authorities (LEAs) fear that the
third partner in the educational endeavour — central government — is
choosing to take to itself additional powers and so disturb the delicate
equilibrium that has existed throughout the development of public
education.

As a result of these difficulties there is a need to re-examine many
different aspects of our system. In line with the greater emphasis given,
in recent times, to the need for accountability, politicians (at central and
local level) are questioning the workings of schools. Governors and
parents, as well as particular pressure groups, are requiring more
information about educational processes. Three particular issues stand
out: the moves, in a few LEAs, to restore a selective system of
secondary schooling; the attempts to achieve public savings which have
led to LEAs being declared 'at risk' by an HMI report; and the various
initiatives on equal opportunities for staff and pupils being undertaken
by LEAs. It is with these initiatives that much of this chapter is
concerned.

Before describing the aims of these initiatives two explanations

1

have to be given. One concerns the term social class: the other is a historical note on the development of the current system of secondary education.

Section One

Social Class

'Social class' is used by researchers as a shorthand label and, like most labels, it is of limited value. In the scale, developed by the Registrars General, occupations are classified into major categories: social class I and II include professional and managerial occupations (about 16 per cent of working population); social class IIIa includes other non-manual workers (31 per cent), and social class IIIb, skilled manual workers (26 per cent); semi-skilled occupations are in social class IV (18 per cent), and unskilled in social class V (about 6 per cent). In London there are slightly larger proportions in non-manual and unskilled occupations and slightly fewer in the skilled and semi-skilled groups. This scale, however, says little about the type of home, the quality of relationships between parents and children and family interests or life style. The use of the term may also serve to emphasize similarities between families leading to stereotypes, where in reality there is considerable variation. Furthermore, the common practice of using only the father's occupation neglects the mother's key role whether or not she is in paid employment.

The term 'working class' is itself emotive. Moreover, because people's social class categories change as their jobs alter, those who move to non-manual occupations are constantly moving out of that class. Further, parents in social classes IV and V may have their most 'mobile' daughters and sons counted in a different group. But, for all these criticisms, social class still seems to measure something and is the best tool we have for seeing if there are important group differences in achievement in various aspects of our society.

Historical Background to the Education Service

The history of public education is not very long. Attendance at elementary school was made compulsory up to the age of 10 only in 1880. Regulations governing free places in grammar schools were introduced in 1907. Free compulsory education for pupils over age 11 was introduced only as a result of the 1944 Act. The Act did not specify 'types of pupils' but merely required local education authorities to provide secondary schools 'sufficient in number, character and equipment to afford for all pupils opportunities for education offering such variety of instruction and training as may be desirable in view of their different ages, abilities and aptitudes' (Education Act, 1944).

1944 Education Act

The Act, although general in its wording, was interpreted (at least implicitly) as accepting the thinking expressed in both the Spens (1938) and the Norwood (1943) reports. This thinking was in favour of providing different types of schools for different types of pupils. The pupils were seen as: those interested in learning for its own sake; those interested in practical/applied rather than academic learning; and those who needed concrete rather than abstract learning. The schools to suit these pupils were seen, respectively, as grammar, technical and secondary modern. As a result of the 1944 Act (and the thinking implicit in its regulations) the tripartite system was created. The selection procedures for entry into the different types of schools made use of group intelligence tests (developed by Godfrey Thompson of Moray House and Cyril Burt, the London County Council (LCC) psychologist from 1913). Underpinning the use of selection procedures was the belief that inequality of opportunity based on the ability of parents to pay for the education of their children would be eliminated. The proponents of the tripartite system aimed to treat children of the same measured ability in the same way and to provide groups of children with an 'equal but different' education, according to their perceived ability and assumed needs.

In reality, the notion of 'equal but different' failed and parity of esteem between the three types of schools was never created. Few technical schools were established and the secondary moderns became the cinderellas of the education service despite providing for the majority of the school population. Even at the start of the tripartite system some educationalists were cautious of the assumptions underlying selection. There was also considerable anxiety about the validity of intelligence testing. Thus, in 1945, the LCC included parental choice and reports from headteachers in the selection procedures. In 1955 attainment tests in English and mathematics were added and, in 1963, the one-day test was abandoned in favour of a primary profile.

Interestingly the London School Plan of 1947 specifically rejected the idea of selection and planned for sixty-four comprehensive schools. The Education Committee of the LCC was influenced, in this decision, by reports of Scottish 'multilateral' and American 'omnibus' schools.

Apart from arguments based on the view that selection procedures were inadequate (or indeed that selection was based on an erroneous view of intelligence) the main criticisms were concerned with evidence that the selection system was biased in favour of middle-class families (see, for instance, Floud *et al* 1956; Jackson and Marsden 1963; and Douglas 1964.)

Criticism of Selection

During the 1960s and 1970s criticism of selection grew more vociferous. A series of government reports drew attention to the waste of underdeveloped talent. Parents — especially in those areas where, for historical reasons, there were smaller numbers of grammar school places — became more insistent in their demands for comprehensive education and these demands resulted in the creation of comprehensive systems. Finally, Anthony Crosland, as Secretary of State for Education and Science, authorized the sending of a circular instructing the remaining LEAs to create comprehensive schools. Most LEAs had already adapted their systems; others began to do so. A few LEAs refused and one contested the powers of central government in the courts. The ILEA, despite the London School Plan of 1947, completed its move to comprehensive education only in 1977 when three former voluntary grammar schools left the system in order in become independent.

Comprehensive Education

The growth of comprehensive education to cover the majority of the nation's children was welcomed by many educationalists. Influenced by the writings of Tawney (1931) they believed that comprehensive schools would produce a greater development of talent than had been accepted by the tripartite system. On the basis of social psychology (Himmelweit, 1952; Jahoda, 1952) they hoped that comprehensive schools would widen the occupational horizons of their pupils. The case studies of researchers like Hargreaves (1967) led to the belief that pupils in comprehensive education would show less of a tendency to mix only with friends of their own social type. Finally, the work of Hoggart (1957) and Turner (1961) led to hopes that pupils would have more flexible views on social class than had been exhibited by those educated under the tripartite system.

These hopes were bold. For many involved in education the growth of comprehensive schools meant an opportunity to break the class bias of the previous system; a bias which had persisted through the 'meritocratic' phase following the 1944 Act.

LEA Initiatives

The 1981 ILEA initiative on achievement, like similar exercises elsewhere, provided the opportunity to reappraise the system of schooling operating in London. It was an opportunity to examine — within an adequately funded and staffed comprehensive system — the relative pattern of achievement of pupils from different backgrounds. (The initiative dealt with three areas: the achievement of pupils coming from working class backgrounds; the achievement of girls; and the achievement of pupils from families of ethnic minorities. Only the first of these areas will be discussed here though there is clearly much overlap between this and the other two.)

As was noted in the initial paper reporting the initiative (ILEA, 1983) there was, underlying this approach, a clear assumption that whilst not all pupils can achieve the same educational level — some are obviously more gifted than others, motivation and interest vary enormously — whole groups should not fall short in their achievement.

Evidence on the Relationship of Social Class and Education

Academic progress

Many different research studies have demonstrated differences in the academic progress of pupils which is related to the social class of their parents. One such study was the longitudinal project carried out by Douglas. This study followed the progress of all the children born within one week in March 1948. Considerable differences in school performance at age 8 were found between children from non-manual and from manual backgrounds (Douglas 1964). Moreover, when the cohort was re-tested at age 11 these differences had increased.

A second cohort study, the National Child Development Study (NCDS), of children born exactly ten years later (March 1958), also found class differences in attainment (Davie *et al*, 1972). Figure 1 shows the proportions of 7 year-old children with poor reading scores.

Figure 1: Children (aged 7) with 'poor' reading scores

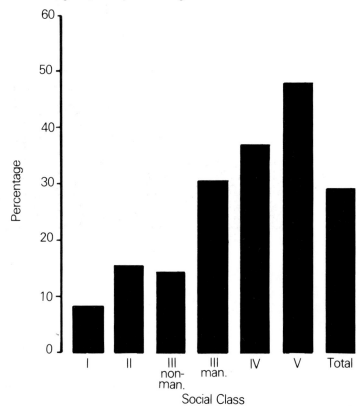

Source: National Child Development Studies (1972)

The proportion of children showing problems in social class V (those with parents who were unskilled) was five times that of social class 1 (those with parents in professional occupations). By the time these children were aged 11, the difference between the groups had doubled and, by the time they were 16, they had widened still further.

A similar — though less pronounced — pattern was found in mathematics.

Figure 2: Children (aged 7) with 'poor' arithmetic scores

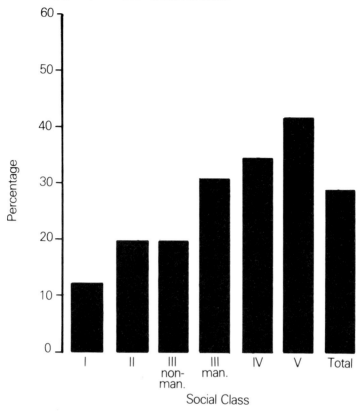

Source: National Child Development Studies (1972)

Whereas only 12 per cent of social class I had poor arithmetic scores, for social class V the figures was 40 per cent. As with reading these differences increased at age 11 and at age 16.

When the researchers asked teachers for recommendations for special educational help in the school or in a special school, class differences were again found.

About 13 per cent of children overall were recommended for special help within the school. For social class I the figure was 4 per cent whilst for social class V it was just under 25 per cent. The numbers recommended as suitable for transfer to special school were much smaller, but the difference between the classes even more accentuated, less than 0.5 per cent for class I and over 6 per cent for class V.

Analyses based on the public examination results of the NCDS cohort have been published recently. Although the focus of the study is

Figure 3: Children (aged 7) needing special educational provision

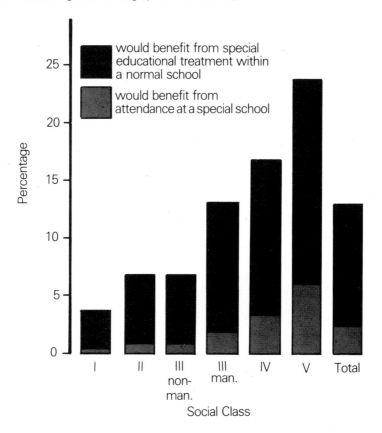

Source: National Child Development Studies (1972)

Table 1: University acceptances (1977/1982)

Social class		% accepted candidates					
		1977	1978	1979	1980	1981	1982
I	Professional/managerial	20.9	21.7	21.9	22.3	24.5	23.9
II	Intermediate	41.2	41.5	42.3	47.8	48.9	49.0
IIIa	Clerical	14.8	14.4	13.4	10.4	9.1	9.1
IIIb	Skilled manual	16.6	16.1	16.3	14.0	12.3	12.2
IV	Semi-skilled manual	5.2	5.2	5.0	4.4	4.2	4.9
V	Unskilled	1.2	1.2	1.0	1.0	1.0	0.9
	TOTAL	100	100	100	100	100	100

Note: Comparison between 1979 and 1980 is not accurate due to changes in coding of occupations

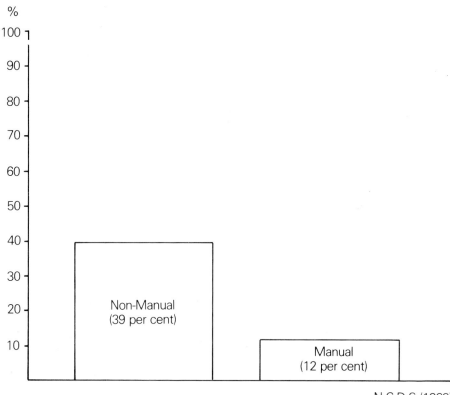

Figure 4: Pupils gaining five high grades in public examinations

Source: National Child Development Studies (1983)

on a comparison of selective and non-selective schooling, assessment of the performance of pupils from different social class backgrounds is possible. Figure 4 shows the perceptions of non-manual and manual groups who gained five 'O' level equivalents.

Similar findings were obtained in the study carried out in London secondary schools in the late 1970s (Rutter *et al*, 1979).

In entry to higher education there are even stronger class differences. Halsey *et al's* (1980) study of successive generations of boys has shown how the chances of a boy from a working class background going to university, despite the increases in provision, were virtually the same as had existed forty years before. The latest data from the University Central Council of Admissions (UCCA) (1982) show that class differences in acceptance rates are substantial.

9

The proportion of accepted candidates from social class V has remained at a low level throughout the period. Likewise, the figure of over 20 per cent for candidates from social class 1 has also remained very stable.

Even when other kinds of higher education are taken into account clear class differences remain, as the following table illustrates.

Table 2: Participation in higher education by social class

Class	1962	1977	Change
Middle	19.5%	27.0%	+7.5%
Working	3.2%	5.0%	+1.8%

Source: Farrant, J. (1981) 'Trends in admissions' in Fulton, O. (Ed.) *Access to Higher Education,* Guildford, SRHE

Farrant's data show that, in 1962, 7.5 per cent of the age-group were participating in higher education. By 1977 this figure had increased to 13 per cent. Most of this increase, however, had been taken up by more from the middle classes (+7.5 per cent). In contrast, although there had been some increase for students with working class backgrounds, this was much more limited (+1.8 per cent).

Using Farrant's data in a more detailed way, it is possible to investigate the class composition of different types of higher education. Table 3 shows an analysis of students in universities, polytechnics and the Open University.

Table 3: Distribution by social class in different types of higher education

	Universities	Polytechnics (FT)	Polytechnics (PT)	Open University
Middle class	70%	64%	51%	47%
Working class	20%	26%	34%	52%
Not classified	10%	10%	15%	0%
All	100%	100%	100%	100%

Source: Ibid

Those from working class backgrounds formed only 20 per cent of the universities student body, 26 per cent of the polytechnic full-time students, 34 per cent of their part-time students, but 52 per cent of the Open University students.

Interestingly, those involved in higher education are beginning to realize the value of student numbers (a lesson falling rolls has taught to school teachers). Williams and Blackstone (1983) have calculated, that if the current pattern of participation remains, there will be a loss of

110,000 students by 1995. In their calculation this is likely to mean the closure of sixteen universities. In contrast, they estimate that if the participation of working class students increased to the level of their middle class peers, places would be needed for a *further* 140,000 students. In this case twenty new universities would be needed.

In summary, throughout the years of primary and secondary schooling the clear class differences in school performance, that emerge as early as age 7, increase. At the stage of entry to higher education there is a massive imbalance in the proportions of candidates from different social classes.

Non-academic matters

Other areas of school life have not been studied as carefully as has academic development. Nevertheless, several investigations have examined the relationship between social class and various non-academic aspects of schooling.

Social Class and Attendance

A number of studies have found evidence of social class differences in attendance patterns (Fogelman, 1976; Tyerman, 1968; Davies, 1980). Davies, for example, found a difference of 7.2 per cent between the attendance of pupils with a non-manual family background, and those from social class V.

Table 4: Absence by parental occupation

Occupational group	% Absence
Non manual	11.3
III manual	16.0
IV	15.7
V	18.5
Unemployed	27.4

Source: Davies, J. (1980) *Perspectives on Attendance*, London, ILEA

This difference of 7.2 per cent was slight, however, compared with a difference of 16.1 per cent between the absence rates of pupils with non-manual family backgrounds, and those whose parents were unemployed.

Of course, attendance at school is likely to be affected by many other influences. ILEA research has drawn attention to the lower rates of absence of pupils with working mothers. Similarly, several ILEA studies have indentified pupils with Caribbean family backgrounds as having *higher* rates of attendance than their peers (see, for example, Davies).

For the majority of pupils, however, it is clear that social class has considerable influence on attendance rates. Whether that is a direct influence (working class parents being less motivated to insist that their children attend school) or an indirect one (pupils with working class backgrounds being less successful in academic life and, therefore, being less committed to the value of schooling) has not yet been resolved satisfactorily.

School Behaviour

The study of school behaviour is extremely complex. Even the definition of disruptive behaviour can pose difficulties (for a full discussion of this topic see Mortimore *et al*, 1984). Because school behaviour is influenced by teacher behaviour and by the general ethos of the school, it is not possible to use behaviour ratings of pupils (carried out by teachers) as a truly independent measure. Where this is done — as in the ILEA Education Priority Index (EPI) measure of school adjustment — social class differences are found but, as some researchers have argued, these differences may, to some extent, also reflect the positive bias of some teachers towards pupils from middle class homes. The EPI data on adjustment to school may be seen in the following table:

Table 5: Social class and adjustment to school

Occupational group	% successful adjustment	% less successful adjusted
Non manual	91.3	8.7
Skilled manual	88.8	11.2
Semi/unskilled	83.0	17.0
Unemployed	76.3	23.7
Not known	83.9	16.1
All	85.6	14.4

Source: EPI (1982)

The relationship of social class to behaviour can also be examined using data from an ILEA study of support centres. Table 6 provides information on the occupational background of parents of a sample of 181 pupils attending support centres. The table includes, for comparative purposes, information on the background of pupils in secondary schools (taken from EPI data).

Table 6: Occupation categories of parents

Occupational group	Centre pupils	ILEA secondary pupils
Non manual	23.2%	30.0%
Skilled manual	26.0%	37.0%
Semi/unskilled	50.8%	33.0%

Source: Mortimore, P. *et al* (1984) *Behaviour Problems in Schools: An Evaluation of Support Centres,* Croom Helm

As can be seen there were *less* pupils with parents in non-manual or skilled occupations in the support centre sample than in the Authority as a whole. There were *more* pupils whose parents were semi- or unskilled.

These two measures are, of course, merely indications that social class is related to school behaviour. Without more detailed data it is not possible to be more specific. The difficulty, as has already been noted, is that school behaviour is not something that can be identified and studied in isolation since it is usually performed in interaction with other pupils or teachers within the social context of a particular school. Studies which have attempted to compare school behaviour as measured by trained observers within different schools, usually have done so with group data which cannot be disaggregated to individuals and so be related to their social class background (see, for example, Rutter *et al*, 1979). Furthermore, it is possible that the same behaviour may even be interpreted quite differently according to the social background of the pupil.

However, despite those somewhat academic points, few teachers would probably disagree with the notion that pupils from working class family backgrounds — who have on average less good attendance and perform, on average, less well in academic tests and examinations — are less likely to see school in a positive light and to behave accordingly. If pupils feel that schools are middle-class institutions, and those with working class backgrounds sense that they are less welcome than some of their peers, it is surely very likely that their behaviour will reflect this view. Although the realization of difference may take time, we know from the case studies of schools that once an 'anti-school' attitude develops there is little chance of succeeding academically

(Hargreaves, 1967; Lacey, 1970; Willis, 1977; Corrigan, 1979; Ball, 1981). Thus, in Ball's study of a comprehensive school, the 'middle-band' pupils — who were more likely to be working class — received ten times as many detentions as a 'top-band' peer, were away twice as often, did only one-third as much homework, and were four times as likely to be late for school. Using an idea from the American psychologist Carol Dweck, it is possible to see pupils from working class backgrounds developing 'learned helplessness' and conforming to the negative stereotypes held by both pupils and teachers (Dweck, 1977). In these circumstances it is not surprising that, in general, pupils from working-class backgrounds leave school sooner than their middle-class peers.

Table 7: Occupation of parents of school leavers and sixth-formers

Occupation group	Leavers	Sixth-formers
Non manual	26%	49%
Skilled manual	47%	33%
Other manual	15%	12%
Unemployed	12%	6%
All	100%	100%

Source: Dean, J. (1982) *Educated Choice at 16*, Research Study Final Report, London, ILEA

The data shown in table 7 is taken from an ILEA study of the educational choices faced by pupils in their last statutory year at school. Nearly half of those choosing to remain at school had parents in non-manual occupations, in contrast to only just over one-quarter of those who had chosen to leave school. Pupils whose parents were unemployed were twice as likely to be amongst the leavers as amongst those staying on.

Section Two

Reasons for the Relationship Between Education and Social Class

What are the reasons for the relationships between education and social class?

Many theories have been suggested for this relationship but hard research evidence is scarce. This is partly because of the enormous difficulties of designing studies which will identify cause and effect in highly complex areas and partly because of the cost of the resources needed to gather reliable data.

What evidence there is can be presented under two main headings:

(i) *individual factors* (material and environmental circumstances and cultural influences);
(ii) *school factors* (teacher attitudes and expectations, school organization, educational resources, examinations and peer group pressures.)

Individual Factors

Health

The relationship between social class and health is well documented (Baxter, 1981; Townsend and Davidson, 1982). Despite the welfare state, babies born to families in the lowest social classes enter the world with less chance of developing into healthy, sturdy children. There are striking differences in birth weight, perinatal mortality rates and childhood accidents (Townsend and Davidson, 1982). Although, each decade, children have tended to get taller, differences between the social classes have remained constant (Tanner, 1969).

Poor vision, impaired hearing and dental decay have also been found to be more common among low income families (Wedge and Prosser, 1973). All of these conditions are likely to affect adversely educational performance.

Poverty

Townsend's major study has indicated the extent of poverty in Britain, a picture which, in view of worsening economic circumstances, is likely to have deteriorated since the author collected his data (Townsend, 1979). Poverty, not surprisingly, was found to be closely correlated with occupational status: the highest incidence being amongst unskilled manual workers and their dependents. Estimates of the number of children living in poverty are difficult to make. Wedge and Prosser suggested — on the basis of their data on 11 year olds — that almost 14 per cent were doing so. By the time the children in their sample were 16 this estimate had dropped to about 12 per cent. However, the educational effects of living in a poor family at the age of 11 appeared to endure, regardless of the situation at 16 (Wedge and Essen, 1982).

Unemployment is also closely related to poverty and to social class. Poor, unemployed parents will have less money to spend on materials and activities to further their children's development and to foster the skills which schools reward. There is also likely to be increased parental stress in poor families which may mean parents are less able to show interest in, or encouragement for, their children. There will be pressure on older children to leave school at the earliest opportunity, even if only to draw unemployment benefit. These young people will be more likely, anyway, to take evening or weekend jobs and so have less time and energy for their studies either at home or at school (MacLennan, 1982).

Housing

Davie *et al* collected information on overcrowding and amenities in the home (hot water, bathroom and indoor lavatory). Their figures showed a remarkable social class trend. Approximately 93 per cent of children from social class I and II were in families with the sole use of the above amenities compared with less than 66 per cent of children in social class V. Poor housing may well affect educational progress as a result of the difficulties of having somewhere quiet to study at home, or because of the lack of a good night's sleep.

Family size

The impact of family size on educational performance tends to be greater among children from working class than from middle class homes (Wedge and Prosser, 1973). In the middle classes, it seems, only those children from a family with four or more offspring are affected adversely. In families from manual occupations children are progressively educationally handicapped with each increase in family size.

One-parent families

Although the evidence is not conclusive, on the whole studies seem to show that, by themselves, single parent families (as a result of either death or divorce) show little association with educational disadvantage (Essen, 1979; Sammons *et al*, 1982).

What does seem to be an important influence is the poverty associated with single parent families. From the evidence available, it would appear that it is not usually the family disruption by itself, but rather, the longer term social and economic adversities frequently associated with the disruption which are important and which have implications for educational attainment (Hinde, 1980).

Cultural Factors

Language

Much attention hs centred on supposed class differences in children's language, and the educational implications of these. During the 1960s and 70s proponents of the 'cultural deprivation' thesis maintained that low achievement by working class children could be attributed to early environment experiences (or lack of them) and different child-rearing practices which resulted in linguistic deficits (Friedman, 1967).

Adherents of the cultural difference theory argued that working-class children had the same ability to reason, and the same language structure as middle-class children, but that there were differences in the ease with which children from different social backgrounds responded to the demands made upon them at school. Bernstein (1977) suggested that differences in early socialization, and in particular in the influence of the mother, had implications for how children responded to school demands.

Tough (1977) maintained that working-class children were not 'linguistically deficient' but that they lacked the encouragement and opportunities to practise their skills. However, research by Tizard *et al* (1980) provides evidence that both middle-class and working-class children talk and are talked to a good deal at home, but that school provides fewer occasions for adult–child conversation than is normally supposed.

Mother-Child Interaction

There is strong evidence that the incidence of depression and neuroticism is higher amongst working-class women than their middle-class counterparts (Rutter, 1976). In their study on the Isle of Wight and in an inner London borough Rutter *et al* (1970) found that emotional disorders were related to environment. In both areas child psychiatric disorders were associated with family disruption, parental illness or criminality, and social-class disadvantage.

Parental Attitudes

The importance of parents' attitudes for childrens' achievement has been well documented in research studies — as have claims of class differences in parental interest in and support for their children's education (Douglas, 1964). The Plowden Committee commissioned a survey of parents of primary school children and found parental attitudes were more strongly related to educational achievement than any other factor (Morton-Williams, 1967).

However, evidence on parental attitudes needs to be treated with caution (Acland, 1980). Lack of interest has often been assumed, but direct evidence from parents suggests that most do not lack interest; rather they are inhibited by lack of self confidence or insufficient knowledge (Tizard *et al*, 1981).

The impact of many of these factors — individual, family, environmental and cultural — is clearly considerable; for many families the effects of a combination of factors (poor housing, poverty and poor health) can be devastating. It is the relationship of low social class to each of the other factors that illustrates its importance as an indicator of disadvantage.

The effect of combinations of factors has been investigated recently in an ILEA study drawing on the 1982 EPI data. Through the construction of a risk index it was possible for us to examine the *chances* of pupils with differing backgrounds being classified in the bottom 25 per cent of candidates taking a measure of general performance in the secondary transfer process. Full details of the analysis are provided in Sammons *et al* (1982) but, briefly, it was clear that the various factors used (eligibility for free meals, large families, one-parent families, low

Table 8: Percentages of pupils affected by different numbers of factors

Number factors	% pupils in VR band 3	% pupils with disturbed behaviour
0	10.8	5.6
1	16.7	9.4
2	25.5	14.7
3	32.2	20.4
4	38.6	25.1
5	49.1	28.6
6	61.5	32.7
7	91.7 (N=12)	42.3 (N=26)
	(N=22, 241)	(N=22, 241)

Source: Sammons, P *et al* (1982) *Educational Pronty Indices — A New Perspective*, ILEA RS868/82

social class, lack of fluency in English, etc) formed a cumulative scale of risk. The effects of this can be seen in the table 8.

As the number of factors experienced by a pupil increases, so does the chance of falling in the bottom 25 per cent of the age group. Similarly, the chance of being rated as having some kind of disturbed behaviour also rises in a linear progression.

Of course, statistics do not, and cannot, convey the picture of human deprivation as graphically as does Harrison (1983) in his description of conditions in Hackney:

> There is no objective way of weighing one type of misery against another. No one can construct an unchallengeable index of total deprivation that would enable us to rank locations in the lower reaches of hell.

It is clear, however, that some progress has been made. One only has to recall Engel's (1892) chilling descriptions of 'the most horrible spot ... known as Little Ireland' in the Manchester of 1845 to realize this. Hackney conditions may be awful but they cannot compete with 'the mass of refuse, offal, and sickening filth ... the atmosphere poisoned by the effluvia ... of a dozen tall factory chimneys and (the people living in) dark wet cellars in measureless filth and stench'. Returning from history to statistics, it is apparent that the strengths of the various individual and family factors are considerable and are likely to explain — to a certain extent — the nature of the relationship of social class to education. It must be remembered, however, that regardless of this relationship, many individual pupils of low social class who have experienced all those disadvantages will prove academically successful. In the same way many advantaged pupils will fail in their schooling regardless of their middle-class background. It is also true there is movement between social classes as Rutter and Madge (1976) and Halsey (1983) have argued. What must be emphasized, however, is that, in terms of the 'chances' of educational success, pupils from middle-class backgrounds have — in general — many advantages.

School Factors

At both primary and secondary levels there have been claims that pupils from different social class backgrounds receive differential treatment from teachers (Rist, 1970; Keddie, 1971). It has also been suggested that knowledge of low socio-economic status and 'deprived' backgrounds may affect, in subtle ways, teachers' expectations and assessments of pupils (Pilling and Pringle, 1978). Barker-Lunn (1970) also found that teachers tended to undervalue the ability of working class children and to overrate the ability of middle-class children.

Teachers' attitudes and expectations may well be influenced by views communicated by other teachers. Fuchs (1968), for example, has discussed how an inexperienced, but well-intentioned rationale that 'in the slum it is the child and the family who fail, but never the school'. Marland (1980) has also warned of good and humane intentions masking 'dangerous attitudes which belittle the possibilities of educational growth for pupils'. However, other studies have found that teachers gave more praise and feedback to low ability groups (Wernstein, 1976) and that there was no evidence of preferential treatment (Croll, 1981).

In addition, there are several studies that show differences in achievement between similar kinds of schools once variations in intake have been taken into account (Rutter *et al*, 1979; Reynolds *et al*, 1976; Edmonds, 1978). However, these researchers generally have found that the more effective schools do not actually alter the social-class patterns of achievement, but rather than they appear to 'jack-up' the attainment of *all* pupils without closing the gap between the classes.

The converse of these findings is, of course, that other schools have negative effects on the achievement of their pupils. How this happens has been hinted at by recent studies of schools, though detailed work documenting the causal influences has still to be carried out.

Among other aspects of schooling noted by researchers as important is the quality of teaching. American research has drawn attention to particularly effective teaching strategies. Although all schools will have a spread of very good, good and less good teachers, in some schools it appears easier to be a 'good teacher' than in others.

It is also likely that, in addition to the skill of the teacher, positive expectations, well-structured courses, good coordination and supervision within teaching departments, and adequate resources and back-ups are also crucial.

Resources

Despite attempts to equalize the distribution of resources, inequalities at national level remain. Pupils from the higher socio-economic groups benefit disproportionately from the available provision (Le Grand, 1982). At local authority level, Howick and Hassani (1980) found evidence that only in London did higher expenditure benefit the disadvantaged. A study of one local authority revealed that the poorest children attended the least well provided schools — 'as the borough responded to government policies . . . the more deprived children were worst affected' (Tunley *et al*, 1979).

Provision for Under 5s

The current system of pre-school care and education can work to the educational disadvantage of children from low socio-economic groups. State nursery education provided by LEAs is free — but is available full-time only in exceptional cases (and then for hours which are of limited value to parents who need to work full-time) — and is rarely sufficient to satisfy local demands. Such a system favours middle-class parents, fewer of whom have both to work full-time. State day care provision (provided under the auspices of the DHSS) is subject to means-tested parental contributions and, even though all-day care is offered, the educational input is slight (Tizard *et al*, 1976). The children in state day care are less likely to be from middle-class families and are more likely to live in 'social priority' areas or be those whose parents (or single parent) work long hours. The result is 'a divided and divisive service' (Hughes *et al*, 1980) in which children most in need of pre-school education, in order to improve their life chances, are least likely to receive it.

Examinations

Whilst the organization and curriculum of secondary schools remain dominated by public examinations it is difficult to see how, even with 'effective' schools, the underachievement of some groups of pupils can be avoided. Examinations — at least of the kind we use now — are highly competitive. Pupils from homes suffering from severe disadvantage will compete with those who, throughout their lives, have enjoyed every possible support. Further, the detailed research by the Schools Council and others into the examination system shows that the mode of assessment may itself be biased in favour of middle class candidates (Schools Council, 1979). Through its essentially competitive nature,

21

the public examinations system will discriminate against pupils who have any social disadvantages (Mortimore and Blackstone, 1982).

To make matters worse, the fact that examinations are rooted in a selective school system means that 'O' level is still favoured over CSE and successful performance commonly is measured by the gaining of five high grades. For many pupils in secondary schools the chances of achieving this level are low. Small wonder that so many pupils give up towards the end of secondary school. Truancy and disruption present alternatives which, for some pupils, must be hard to resist.

Peer Influence

Strong though the influence of school undoubtedly is, the power of the pupil peer group is at least as strong, if not stronger. There have been few good studies of peer influence among girls. This is mainly because of the difficulties of studying the private interactions of a social subgroup. However, the conflict between the values of the grammar school and the peer group culture have been described in Willmott's (1969) study of adolescents in the East End.

The 'delinquent' subcultures which Hargreaves (1967) describes suggest that, for those pupils for whom school is not a place where they experience success, the peer culture will be especially important. Willis' study of working class boys describes their 'entrenched general and personalized opposition to authority' and their struggle to defeat the aims of the school.

We have drawn here on a number of different studies to suggest ways in which social class can influence education. Inevitably much of the evidence has been general and has not provided clear guidance on the various mechanisms involved. Further detailed research studies into the mechanisms of this influence are needed so that teachers can attempt to counter its effects. In the meantime various possible strategies must be tried and some of these are listed in the next section.

Section Three

Towards a More Equitable System

The complexity of the factors underlying social class differences in achievement means that there can be no simple response by the education service. Teachers, of course, cannot change pupils' homes, nor should they try to do so. Teachers cannot (by themselves) effect the large-scale social and economic changes which would help mitigate factors associated with class differences in education. However, the research on school differences and school effectiveness suggests that the education system can increase or decrease pupils' chances of achievement and that those within the system are in a position to exert influence. It is essential, therefore, that all those involved in education do respond. How best this can be done is not clear and a variety of approaches needs to be tried. Some approaches will involve individual teachers and their school colleagues re-examining their own practices, others will seek to change the structure of our current system of secondary education. Both approaches are essential. Changes in structure which ignore those working in schools will surely fail, as will exhortations to individual teachers to overcome, by their efforts alone, the effects of social disadvantage.

How Teachers Can Help

The progress of *all* groups of pupils needs to be monitored carefully so that differences in achievement can be identified early and remedial action taken. Conscious efforts need to be made to raise teachers' expectations of the achievement of pupils from working-class homes in order to reduce the influence of negative stereotypes. Books and learning materials need to be suitable for all pupils and not represent a monocultural view of society. Extra learning opportunities, such as homework clubs and revision courses, may well help pupils who have poor facilities for study at home.

School Self-Evaluation

The debate on accountability in education has served to focus attention on the techniques of self-evaluation in order to enable teachers to be more critical of their performance, both individually and as a group. In 1980 approximately seventy local education authorities were involved in some kind of evaluation (Elliott, 1980). By now there are undoubtedly more and the overall number of schools involved must be enormous. In London, for example, all primary and secondary schools carry out annual reviews which include some self-evaluation.

Self-evaluation does, of course, take time. If teachers are devoting efforts to this it is likely to be at the expense of some other activity and, naturally, they will be anxious that it is time well spent. In our view the critical conditions for success in self-evaluation are: guaranteed confidentiality; the opportunity to develop a trusting relationship with a peer; and, within the climate created by these two conditions, honest feedback.

Self-evaluation can take place in the individual classroom (see for example, Open University, 1981) but perhaps of greater relevance here is the concept of *school* self-evaluation. This is more than an aggregation of the world of individual teachers: it includes the monitoring of the general effects of the institution on pupils (and staff); the pastoral arrangements; the corporate life of the school and many other areas of school life which do not necessarily take place within a classroom (see for example, ILEA, 1977; Mortimore, 1982).

In our view changes that are introduced as a result of some form of self-evaluation are far more likely to be maintained than others whose introduction has been negotiated by an outsider. This is not to say that outsiders have no role but rather that their role may be more valuable when they use their skills to help the teachers to increase their own insights.

The work of ILEA curriculum support teams has also included modest attempts at changing schools. The teams operate in schools with high levels of socially disadvantaged children. They aim to stimulate discussion and to negotiate development of the curriculum in ways designed to improve the quality of children's learning. In terms of changing institutions, the evaluation carried out so far suggests that the value of the approach is in enthusing teachers and in initiating the (admittedly lengthy) process of getting them to question and look closely at what they are teaching and at what children are learning (Jayne, 1981).

Parent Involvement

There is a growing body of evidence to suggest that the aim of equality of educational opportunity can be furthered by fostering parents' interest in, and increasing their knowledge of, education. The results, for example, of the Haringey Reading Project (Tizard *et al*, 1980), of similar work in Rochdale and in the ILEA PACT Project in Hackney demonstrate the potential for improving the performance of children from working class homes by involving parents (with teachers) in assisting their own children's reading (Griffiths, 1983).

Structural Change

The key to structural change, in our opinion, must lie in the reform of the examination system though change is also needed in the curriculum and organization of schools. Examination reform will not be achieved simply by the merging of CSE and 'O' level, but will require a much more imaginative response. Criticisms of the examination system have been well documented and will not be repeated in detail here (Mortimore and Mortimore, 1984). It is clear, however, that in view of the lack of comparability between syllabuses, boards and modes, examination grades are very crude indicators of achievement. It is also clear that traditional papers — still used in most examinations — favour memory and repetition of previously rehearsed arguments, rather than other skills. Over and above these weaknesses it is also surely obvious that any system which, for the majority of candidates, produces a level of achievement regarded by many as a 'failure', needs to be reassessed.

Moves towards devizing alternative forms of assessment are already under way. The developments of profiles and of graded assessments are, as yet, at an early stage, and considerable technical problems have to be overcome. Yet the opportunity to adopt a more encompassing system, building on what the majority of pupils *can do* rather than pinpointing what they cannot do, exists.

Profiles, offering a broad, longer-term picture of a pupil's development, with a component contributed by the pupil, are capable of providing considerably more information to all interested parties than can a GCE or CSE certificate. A wide range of skills and achievements for all pupils can be recognized and rewarded.

Graded assessments present different opportunities. They can be progressive, offer short-term goals and do not depend necessarily on statistical norms. These characteristics are of great significance when they are compared to the drawbacks of the current system where public examinations are not progressive but are taken by most pupils immediately prior to leaving school.

The ILEA is developing a London Record of Achievement. This will consist of a portfolio containing the results of graded assessments and other examinations and a profile compiled by teachers and pupils. Similar to the London portfolio is the Oxford Certificate of Educational Achievement (OCEA) currently being devized by the Oxford Delegacy of Local Examinations and the Oxford University Department of Educational Studies, in collaboration with a number of local authorities.

In combination, profiles and graded assessments could meet all the criteria and fulfil all the functions of the current system — and in most cases do so more efficiently. For this to happen, however, a broader concept of ability — one which embraced a range of personal skills and which permitted more diverse application of knowledge — would need to be accepted.

We believe that three advantages could accrue from such a move. First, the logic accepted in the principle of comprehensive education would be furthered by the transfer of social selection (already transferred from age 11 to age 16) to the post-school stage. Second, the advantages for schools, in no longer being a part of the process of failure, could be considerable and, as a result, much of the painful conflict that is currently manifest between failing pupils and their teachers might be reduced. Third, we believe that by removing the mechanism of social selection to an older age group the influence of background factors of family and social class might be reduced. The older those being selected, the more likely that individual talents motivation, skills and achievements would be considered and the more likely that these would reflect the striving of the individual rather than their background.

These three advantages, in our opinion, justify change. They will not, however, provide a panacea for all difficulties. For example, the problem, elegantly expounded by Hargreaves, of how suitable is the standard secondary curriculum, remains to be solved in other ways (Hargreaves, 1982).

At present, for most secondary schools, the curriculum is based upon the study of separate, traditional subjects. Whilst this may have been entirely appropriate for the selective schools of earlier days it is, we suggest, inappropriate for young people in the 1980s. However, attempts at reform, such as the introduction of social education courses, have frequently failed. This was mainly because courses were not introduced across the board but were restricted to 'less academic' and frequently low social class pupils. As a result, the very courses that were introduced to *help* pupils became the instruments that distinguished them from their peers and institutionalized their failure. Perhaps it is now time to think of a curriculum that does prepare all young people for the lives that face them. This could include: preparation for work, or for extended periods without paid employment; preparation for adult human relationships (including parenting); and preparation for the scientific and technological applications that are likely to feature in all our lives.

Closely related to examinations and the curriculum is the organization of secondary schools. At present this is based on age-related teaching groups. Whilst administratively and, perhaps, socially this may have advantages, in other ways it is unhelpful. There is no opportunity for 'catch-up'. If pupils fail to learn because of illness, lack of attention, personal difficulties or any other reason, it is extraordinarily difficult for them to make up the lost ground. These pupils tend to fall further and further behind their peers and may give up altogether the attempt to catch up.

These are but three areas of possible change in the structure of our secondary school system. There are others, but it is to these we attach the highest priority. Such changes imply a radical reshaping of secondary schools as we know them, and require a rethinking of the teacher's role. The benefit would lie in the freeing of teacher energy and in the more open opportunities for pupils. In these circumstances, hopefully, underachievement by pupils from working-class backgrounds would be less inevitable than under the present system.

This is the challenge facing educators. That the grip social class holds on educational achievements can be loosened is clear from the study of other societies and other educational systems. In our view it is essential that it happens in this country too. We see the present circumstances as opportune for change. The social pressures described at the start of this chapter, the rising tide of criticisms of public examinations, and the increasing attacks on the comprehensive system all, in different ways, contribute to the need for heads, teachers, and others involved in the educational system, to reassess the part played by schools in the perpetuation of the influence of social class.

References

ACLAND, H. (1980) 'Research as stage management: the case of the Plowden Committee', in BULMER, M (Ed.) *Social Research and Royal Commissions*, George Allen and Unwin.

BALL, S. (1981) *Beachside Comprehensive*, Cambridge, Cambridge University Press.

BARKER-LUNN, J. (1970) *Streaming in the Primary School*, Windsor, NFER.

BERNSTEIN, B. (1977) 'Class and pedagogies: visible and invisible' in KARABEL,

J. and HALSEY, A. (Eds) *Power and Ideology in Education*, Oxford, Oxford University Press.

BLAXTER, M. (1981) *The Health of Children*, Heinemann.

CONSULTATIVE COMMITTEE TO THE BOARD OF EDUCATION (1938) *Secondary Education* (the Spens Report), London, HMSO.

CORRIGAN, P. (1979) *Schooling the Smash Street Streets*, Macmillan.

CROLL, P. (1981) in SIMON, B. and WILCOCKS, J. (Eds) *Research and Practice in the Primary Classroom*, Routledge.

DAVIE, R., BUTLER, N. and GOLDSTEIN, H. (1972) *From Birth to Seven*, Longman.

DAVIES, J. (1980) *Perspectives on Attendance*, London, ILEA.

DEAN, J. (1982) *Education Choice at 16*, Research Study Final Report, London, ILEA.

DOUGLAS, J.W.B. (1964) *The Home and the School*, London, MacGibbon and Kee.

DWECK, C. (1977) 'Learned helplessness and negative evaluation', *Education*, 19, 2.

EDMONDS, R. et al (1978) *Search for Effective Schools*, Harvard University Center for Urban Schools.

ELLIOTT, G. (1980) *Self-evaluation and the Teacher I and II*, Hull, University of Hull.

ENGELS, F. (1892) *The Condition of the Working Class in England* (1976 edn), Panther.

ESSEN, J. (1979) 'Living in one-parent families: income and expenditure', *Poverty*, 40.

FARRANT, J. (1981) 'Trends in admissions', in FULTON, O. (Ed) *Access to Higher Education*, Guildford, SRHE.

FLOUD, J., HALSEY, A. and MARTIN, F. (1956) *Social Class and Education Opportunity*, Heinemann.

FOGELMAN, K. (1976) *Britain's Sixteen-year-olds*, National Children's Bureau.

FRIEDMAN, N. (1967) 'Cultural deprivation: a commentary in the sociology of knowledge', *Journal of Educational Thought*, 1, 2.

FUCHS, E. (1968) 'How teachers learn to help children fail', *Trans-Action*, September.

GRIFFITHS, A. (1983) *PACT — Ways Forward*, Report of the PACT Conference, 6 July, Stoke Newington School.

HALSEY, A. (1983) 'Growing up unequal', *Times Educational Supplement*, 16 September.

HALSEY, A., HEATH, A. and RIDGE, J. (1980) *Origins and Destinations*, Clarendon Press.

HARGREAVES, D. (1967) *Social Relations in a Secondary School*, London, Routledge and Kegan Paul.

HARGREAVES, D. (1982) *The Challenge for the Comprehensive School: Culture, Curriculum and Community*, Routledge and Kegan Paul.

HARRISON, P. (1983) *Inside the Inner City*, Pelican.

HIMMELWEIT, H. (1952) 'The view of adolescents on some aspects of class structure', *British Journal of Sociology*, 3.

HINDE, R. (1980) 'Family influences' in RUTTER, N. (Ed.) *Scientific Foundations of Developmental Psychology*, Heinemann Medical Books.

HOGGART, R. (1957) *The Use of Literacy*, Chatto and Windus.

HOWICK, C. and HASSANI, H. (1980) 'Education spending: primary', *CES Review* 5; and 'Education spending: secondary', *CES Review*, 8.

HUGHES, M. *et al* (1980) *Nurseries Now*, Penguin.

ILEA (1983) 'Race, sex and class I', *Achievement in Schools*.

ILEA INSPECTORATE (1977) *Keeping the School under Review*, London, ILEA.

JACKSON, B. and MARSDEN, D. (1963) *Education and the Working Class*, Routledge and Kegan Paul.

JAHODA (1952) 'Job attitude and job choice among secondary modern school children', *Occupational Psychology*.

JAYNE, E. (1981) 'Primary Curriculum Support Team Project (ILEA)', *Report No. 2 RS772/81 and No. 3 RS778/81*.

KEDDIE, N. (1971) 'Classroom knowledge', in YOUNG, M.F.D. (Ed.) *Knowledge and Control*, Collier Macmillan.

LACEY, C. (1970) *Hightown Grammar: The School as a Social System*, Manchester, Manchester University Press.

LE GRAND, J. (1982) 'The distribution of public expenditure on education', *Economic*, spring.

MACLENNAN, E. (1982) *Child Labour in London*, Low Pay Unit.

MARLAND, M. (1980) *Education for the Inner City*, Heinemann.

MORTIMORE, J. and BLACKSTONE, T. (1982) *Disadvantage and Education*, Heineman.

MORTIMORE, J. and MORTIMORE, P. (1984) *Secondary School Examinations: The Helpful Servants not the Dominating Master*, London, Bedford Way Paper, University of London Institute of Education.

MORTIMORE, P. (1982) 'School self-evaluation', in GALTON, M. and MOON, R. (Eds) *Changing Schools . . . Changing Curriculum*, Harper Row.

MORTIMORE, P., DAVIES, J., VARLAAM, A. and WEST, A. (1984) *Behaviour Problems in Schools: An Evaluation of Support Centres*, Croom Helm.

MORTON-WILLIAMS, R. (1967) 'The 1964 national survey among parents of primary school children', *Plowden Report 2, Research and Surveys*, London, HMSO.

OPEN UNIVERSITY (1981) 'A continuing education course for teachers', *Curriculum in Action: An Approach to Evaluation*, Milton Keynes, Open University Press.

PILLING, D. and PRINGLE, M. (1978) *Controversial Issues in Child Development*, Paul Elek.

REYNOLDS, D. and MURGATROYD, S. (1977) 'The sociology of schooling and the absent pupil: the school as a factor in the generation of truancy', in CARROLL, H. (Ed.) *Absenteeism in South Wales: Studies of Pupils, Their Homes and Their Secondary Schools*, Swansea, University College.

RIST, R. (1970) 'Student social class and teacher expectations: the self-fulfilling prophecy in ghetto education', *Harvard Educational Review*, 40.

RUTTER, M. (1976) 'Prospective studies to investigate behavioural change', in STRAUSS, J., BATIGIAN, H. and ROSS, M. (Eds) *Methods of Longitudinal Research in Psychology*, Plenum.

RUTTER, M., MAUGHAM, B., MORTIMORE, P. and OUSTEN, J. (1979) *Fifteen*

Thousand Hours: Secondary Schools and Their Effects on Children, London, Open Books.

RUTTER, M. and MADGE, N. (1976) *Cycles of Disadvantage*, Heinemann.

RUTTER, M., TIZARD, J. and WHITMORE, K. (Eds) (1970) *Education, Health and Behaviour*, Longman.

SAMMONS, P., KYSEL, F. and MORTIMORE, P. (1982) *Educational Priority Indices — A New Perspective*, ILEA RS868/82.

SCHOOLS COUNCIL (1979) 'Comparability in examinations', *Occasional Paper 1*, Schools Council Forum on Comparability.

SECONDARY SCHOOLS EXAMINATIONS COUNCIL (1943) *Curriculum and Examinations in Secondary Schools* (the Norwood Report), London, HMSO.

SHIPMAN, M. (1980) 'The limits of positive discrimination', in MARLAND, M. (Ed.) *Education for the Inner City*, Heinemann.

TANNER, J. (1969) 'Relation of body size, intelligence scores and social circumstances', in MUSSEN, P. *et al* (Eds) *Trends and Issues in Development Psychology*, Holt, Rinehart and Winston.

TAWNEY, R. (1931) *Equality*, Unwin.

TIZARD, B., CARMICHAEL, H., HUGHES, M. and PINKERTON, G. (1980) 'Four year olds talking to mothers and teachers', in HERSON, L. and BERGER, M. (Eds) *Language and Language Disorders in Childhood*, Pergamon Press.

TIZARD, B., MORTIMORE, J. and BURCHELL, B. (1981) *Involving Parents in Nursery and Infant Schools*, Grant McIntyre.

TIZARD, J., MOSS, P. and PERRY, J. (1976) *All Our Children*, Temple Smith/New Society.

TIZARD, J., SCHOFIELD, W. and HEWISON, J. (1982) 'Collaboration between teachers and parents in assisting childrens reading', *British Journal of Educational Psychology*, 52.

TOUGH, J. (1977) *Development of Meaning*, Allen and Unwin.

TOWNSEND, P. (1979) *Poverty in the United Kingdom*, Penguin.

TOWNSEND, P. and DAVIDSON, N. (1982) *Inequalities in Health: The Black Report*, Pelican.

TUNLEY, P., TRAVERS, T. and PRATT, J. (1979) *Depriving the Deprived*, Kogan Page.

TURNER, R. (1961) 'Modes of social ascent through education' HALSEY, A. *Education, Economy and Society*.

TYERMAN, M. (1968) *Truancy*, London, University of London Press.

UNIVERSITY CENTRAL COUNCIL ON ADMISSIONS (UCCA) (1982) *Statistical Supplement to the Nineteenth Report*.

WEDGE, P. and ESSEN, J. (1982) *Children in Adversity*, Pan Books.

WEDGE, P. and PROSSER, N. (1973) *Born to Fail?* Arrow Books.

WERNSTEIN, R. (1976) 'Reading group membership in first grade: teacher behaviour and pupil experience over time', *Journal of Educational Psychology*, 68, 1.

WILLIAMS, G. and BLACKSTONE, T. (1983) *Response to Adversity*, Guildford, SRHE.

WILLIS, P. (1977) *Learning to Labour*, Farnborough, Saxon House.

WILLMOTT, P. (1969) *Adolescent Boys of East London*, Penguin.

Core Curriculum Revisited*

Malcolm Skilbeck

During the 1970s and into the 80s a recurrent theme in curriculum policy debates in many English speaking countries has been the need for and nature of a common or core curriculum. The case made by the Department of Education and Science, through both its administrative and inspectorial sub-cultures, for a national core defined as an amalgamation of subjects and areas of experience has been one of the best sustained and most comprehensive contributions to the debate. But in Australia, Canada and the United States there have also been significant policy statements and, as the OECD study of basic education showed, even many countries with a long tradition of central direction of the curriculum were beginning to take a close interest in the same kinds of themes as were favoured in the English speaking debate. These included the adequacy of the core for all students in secondary schooling, the balance of its component parts, the relevance of what has been taught viewed from changing socio-economic and political perspectives, and the ability or preparedness of the teaching profession to present core learnings in a manner that seemed to capture the interests or meet the needs of youth.

Not surprisingly, initiatives by central government and by national agencies funded from government sources were seen by many educationalists as an excessive reaction to public criticism of schooling — especially of the back-to-basics kind — and to constitute an unwelcome intrusion into territory thought to be the exclusive province of local authorities, schools and individual teachers. In addition to these kinds of criticisms, more sophisticated attacks have come from academics. Thus, the move towards core curriculum was described as

* Reprinted (with minor changes) from *Forum*, 26, 1 autumn 1983

an 'impossible' enterprise since it presupposed a non-existent social consensus; the formulations of aims and directions were characterized as confused and impoverished; and the core learnings proposed were said to represent yet another attempt to impose on schooling the traditions, values and socio-cultural assumptions of the elites in power at the time.

Contrasts were drawn between, on the one hand, the so-called grass roots movements of school-based curriculum development, local initiatives and the quest for variety, teachers as researchers, action research and participatory and communitarian development and, on the other, heavy handed recentralization, reactionary politics and so-called power-coercive strategies of change.

In England and Wales, the National Union of Teachers, in its submission to the House of Commons Select Committee on Education and Science, denied the Department of Education and Science the right to determine national needs and declared its resistance to any curriculum policies which might seem to challenge the teacher's right to determine the curriculum. This was an echo of the arguments surrounding the establishment of the Schools Council in the mid '60s'.

More recently, the government's determination to finish off the Schools Council by withdrawing funds and establishing two new, separate nominated national agencies, one for secondary examinations and the other for school curriculum, has been widely condemned as further evidence of a determination to consolidate power over educational policy into central government and its agencies. Practically no-one in the country's educational service — publicly at any rate — has been prepared to concede that there may be a case that at least deserves examining, for replacing the Council with new agencies. Probably this is because of the manner in which the Secretary of State for Education and Science unilaterally declared his intention to terminate the Council, which had always offered itself as a partnership of central and local government and the teachers. Few curriculum analysts and commentators have begun the much needed task of constructing new interpretative frameworks, or considering the implications of the changes that are undoubtedly upon us. Even those who have, over the years, advocated a compulsory or common curriculum for all, have severely criticized the trend of events insofar as the Department of Education and Science has been a major instrument in forcing the core issue.

We are overdue for a calm and reflective reconsideration of the relationships within the education service itself, between schools and local authorities and between schools, parents, and communities and local authorities and central government and between the various agencies and groups that can reasonably claim some role in curriculum policy making.

As a first step, we need greater clarity about some of the key terms in the curriculum debate than exists at present. First, the term core curriculum. Commonly used by schools to describe those courses which are required of all students in a given institution, core curriculum has a rather different meaning when used in national policy discussions. There, it refers to those programmes, courses or learning opportunities in which all students of a given age or stage in the education system are expected to take part. Notice that in both cases it's the planned, intended or provided curriculum we are talking about and this is important since there is a considerable gap both at school and at system level between the intention of the policy makers, providers and teachers and the curriculum as experienced by the students. In recognition of this, *The Practical Curriculum*[7], published by the Schools Council hard on the heels of the Department's policy document, *The School Curriculum*, (and delayed in publication at the Department's request so that theirs could come out first) used the term 'effective curriculum', that is the curriculum as experienced by the student or, more precisely, what the student 'takes' from the learning experiences provided by the school. These are not just verbal niceties (nor are they precise concepts which can be readily interrelated in an analysis of the curriculum process from intention to realization) but are matters of some importance when we try to work out what is meant by the term core curriculum.

Is the core — whether at school or national system — or local authority level — the planned, stated, prespecified learnings? Or is it the school's realization of these broadly stated learnings (often put in the form of generalizations about areas of experience) in its own plans and programmes, or is it the set of learnings held in common by all students as a result of their engagement with syllabuses, classroom materials and the activities of teachers?

If a theory of core curriculum is advanced, as in the Australian Curriculum Development Centre's *A Core Curriculum for Australian Schools*[8], which presupposes a central determining role for schools, there are several important consequences both for the theory of core curriculum and for the debate over control. First, in that document, core is essentially a proposal that schools in planning their curricula and organizing their learning programmes, ensure that all students, over a prolonged period of schooling, should have access to defined areas and aspects of contemporary culture. If these are to be thought of as areas of experience, in the style of the HMI documents after Hirst, Phenix (and perhaps Cassirer)[9], then it is experience as a socio-cultural category we are addressing. For example, although science exists and may be taught as a 'subject' with its own logical structure of concepts, its methods of enquiry and distinctive forms of validation, and its accumulated organized content of facts, theories techniques and ideas, it also exists and may be taught as a set of cultural phenomena. Let us consider what that might mean.

First, we shall need to locate, define and describe science as a way of life, with a history, a set of social and economic relations, practical as well as theoretical problems to solve. Second, it means treating science as a human, social enterprise with a variety of relations with other human, social enterprises rather than as a self-contained intellectual system with its applications (for example, in technology). That is, it constitutes a problem as well as a resource for other spheres; for example, physics and electricity generation through controversial nuclear power stations, or human genetics and the moral dilemmas of genetic engineering. Third, the cultural approach means seeing areas of experience as networks of subject-subject relations, not as subject-object relations. Simply put, the curriculum task is not to amass new subject matter or update the old, structure it and present it for learning in the form of attractive materials. Our task instead, is to concentrate on the expectations, meanings, aspirations, values and understandings of the learner, treating his or her engagement in which learning is not conceived as ingestion but as the construction and reconstruction of meanings and values. The material or subject matter of learning is, on this analysis and as Dewey[10] long ago observed, a resource.

Now what is the connection between all this and the debate over core curriculum? There has been a widespread assumption that advocates of core curriculum are, in various artful ways, trying to enforce the compulsory teaching of particular subjects in all the nation's schools. Unfortunately, some of the DES utterances would seem to support this interpretation. Even the Inspectorate's proposals for an 'areas of experience' approach gives the impression that we are still in the realm of the transmission of organized bodies of subject matter. These interpretations are not at all surprising given the grip of academic and quasi-academic subjects on the school curriculum and the popularity of naive transmission and reproduction theories among both traditionally minded teachers and many contemporary sociologists of education.

A necessary step, therefore, in clarifying our concept of core curriculum is to distinguish it, on the one hand, from a thinly disguised advocacy of central control over schools and, on the other, from a new version of the subject-centred curriculum. I hope to show, now, how these distinctions may be made.

The table illustrates one concept of core which assumes a central role for schools in curriculum making and acknowledges that subject *matter* is still a major resource in curriculum despite the criticism of the subject-dominated curriculum. Let us assume, first, that it makes sense in our educational system for the school itself to choose, plan, organize and teach its own curriculum. The school does seem to have the legally determined authority to do this, it is provided with appropriate (if not always adequate) resources, in the way of a trained professional staff, physical plant and equipment, materials, specialist advice and ancillary services, and it has the general expectation, frequently confirmed and reinforced, that this is indeed a proper responsibility. Let us assume, next, that while the school principal is the single most important locus of this authority, responsibility and power, his or her exercise of it is contingent on a complex series of negotiations and other relationships with the governing body, the parents, and the teaching staff and students. In other words, the school, for purposes of curriculum making, cannot be reduced to the principal or indeed even to the principal plus teaching staff.

Let us assume next that in making the curriculum and teaching it, the school will be variously influenced and constrained, not only by such specific items as — in secondary education — external examinations, the expectations of further and higher education, the educational achievements of feeder schools and so forth but also by an assortment of vaguely defined but nonetheless real social and cultural forces, such as beliefs and expectations about good order, about what is suitable — or more often not suitable — to teach and so forth.

Given these three assumptions, how do national statements about the aims for and perspectives on core curriculum relate to the school? To put the question the other way round, would schools benefit in their own processes of curriculum review, evaluation and development from nationally formulated proposals regarding what all students, in all schools, should have available by way of a general curriculum framework?

Table 1: Core curriculum and the school
(Core is constructed with nine areas of experience, by schools. It is expressed as school-determined learning processes within these areas, and in terms of learning environments or situations.)

Level 1	Core Curriculum as a set of general aims and areas of experiences, nationally defined (broad guidelines):

Arts and crafts	Moral and values education
Communication	Scientific and technological studies
Environmental studies	Social and cultural studies
Health education	
Mathematical reasoning and applications	Work, leisure and life style

Level 2	Interpreted and adapted by schools into specified processes of learning for all students in each of the above areas
Level 3	These learnings provided for in planned learning environments organized by and through schools.
Assessment:	Single subject, external examinations at 16+, 17+, 18+, or profiles, incorporating an element of external assessment and moderation?

Before answering this question, I should mention that in respect of a number of crucial variables (or what are believed to be crucial variables) in the educational process we quite readily accept national norms. Thus, in examinations, there has been a long-standing move towards greater consistency of requirements (as for example the work of the Schools Council's Forum on Comparability for 'A' Level Syllabuses). Now, there is an acceptance of the case for unifying the CSE and GCE 'O' level exams into a single GCSE. Alternatively, critics of the examination system want a system of profiles but even where they are proposed at school or local authority level it is recognized that there is at least a problem of consistency of demand and presentation which, if not resolved, could spell defeat for the movement.

In other areas, too, we don't hesitate to seek (even where we don't always achieve) national norms, most conspicuously in teacher/pupil ratios, standards of school lighting, heating, pupil space, playgrounds and basic equipment. Reactions to the annual reports by HMI on the state of educational provision have quite rightly centred on the inequalities and the real deprivation of education opportunity consequent on the different rates of local authority spending for pupils in schools in England and Wales.

Here, too, there seems to be a presumption of a desirable norm or a national minimum.

There is much to be said for giving schools greater freedom in the disposal and management of resources and the case has been frequently argued, usually by the more enterprising of our heads and the occasional chief officer. Yet we must not ignore the possible consequences of this freedom for all schools and all children. In some schools, greater freedom from constraints for principals may mean less freedom for students in learning opportunities. In other words, the idea of a national norm, as the Fabians long ago pointed out, is in part to ensure a platform of provision and opportunity for all citizens or future citizens. The argument for freedom of choice for some cannot be addressed in isolation from its consequences for the freedom of opportunity for others.

To return to the core curriculum issue, we may see this move towards national statements on core as a series of steps or proposals. I shall state each of these in turn and comment briefly.

1   Core curriculum proposals are a response to public and political misgivings about the quality of schooling, in particular about standards of attainment in 'fundamentals'.

   Comment: Much of the criticism is unsatisfactory yet it cannot be ignored by administrators. The criticism ought not, however, to be taken at face value, nor can we accept the popular definition of the fundamentals of learning since it is educationally weak and if acted upon would narrow and distort education. Educators need to take a yet more active part in school-community dialogue over 'what is basic and fundamental in the curriculum'.

2   Core curriculum can be usefully formulated by central policy makers in the form of broad guidelines about what subjects to teach, themes to emphasize, and ways of teaching.

   Comment: This approach characterizes not only *The School Curriculum* (and even more *A Framework for the School Curriculum*, the White Paper which preceded it) but also the steadily expanding, more subtle and more pervasive recent work of the Inspectorate. Widespread suspicion and hostility have been engendered and ought not to be left to fester. We have to re-open the core curriculum debate.

3   Following the publication of Circulars 6/81 and 9/83 and the earlier request by DES that LEAs should review and report

on their curriculum policies, schools have been engaged in reviewing their curricula. These reviews do not require the formulation of core curriculum policies. Schools are expected to work within the aims outlined for all schools in *The School Curriculum.*

Comment: *The School Curriculum* has an authoritative force but it is difficult to know whether serious notice is being taken of it by schools. The circulars are a typical administrative follow through and are not the end of the affair. We may expect, in the years ahead, further moves from administrators and inspectorate to bring about greater coherence and consistency — if not a fully worked out core approach — in school curricula. There are weaknesses in the 'review and evaluate' strategy since review and evaluation even when honestly conducted can leave many problems and shortcomings untouched, that is discovered but not acted on; schools cannot be assumed to have either the capacity or commitment to move to the next step, which is development. This point is pertinent, too, to the emerging LEA review and evaluation documents.

4   Further guidelines and circulars pointing up the value of a national core approach may be anticipated (if the Department keeps up the momentum of the past five years).

Comment: On previous form, and in prevailing political and economic climates, these may be expected to generate further resistance or be treated with indifference by significant parts of the teaching profession. We need to work towards a better understanding of just how what have appeared to many commentators as irreconcilable — namely local initiative and responsibility and a national framework of aims and core learnings — may be interrelated in a single strategy.

In conclusion, the argument of this paper has been that there is value in a move towards national core curriculum even though several difficulties and changes have been noted. The most serious problem, now, is that we have no forum, centre or institutional setting wherein the debate can be resumed and dialogue can occur. There are, by contrast, any number of separate sites each occupied by a distinct interest group. I have suggested elsewhere the need for a national forum, now that the Schools Council (which did not, incidentally, ever manage to develop its own ideas about the whole, common or core curriculum) has been replaced by bodies whose acceptability to important parts of the education profession has been jeopardized by the manner of their establishment.

If we cannot be optimistic about the national forum idea, at least the education profession itself, through its numerous voluntary agencies and media of communication and debate, ought to take time over the next few years to address the still unanswered questions:

(i)   Are there learnings which we can characterize as basic and fundamental for all students?
(ii) Can we reach agreement about what they are?
(iii) How do we best organize schooling to achieve them?

These questions, of course, even if consistently addressed, cannot be answered once and for all. Various attempts have been made in recent years, but not even their proponents — of whom I have been one — would suggest that the attempts are any more than introductory sketches of philosophies, politics and programmes of core curriculum.

One of the greatest defects in the official versions of core curriculum has been the neglect of the dynamics of culture and, as a consequence of the processes as distinct from the templates of education. Perhaps it is this, rather than the fact of central government intervention, that has constituted the sticking point for so many in education. If so, there is now a challenge to educators to locate core curriculum analysis in terms, not just of areas of experience, but of learning processes and type of learning environments which may best sustain those processes.

Notes

1 Recent statements include Department of Education and Science (1981) *The School Curriculum*, London, HMSO; and Her Majesty's Inspectorate (1980) *A View of the Curriculum*, London, HMSO.
2 This international movement is documented in SKILBECK, M. (1982) *A Core Curriculum for the Common School*, an inaugural lecture, London. University of London Institute of Education.
3 Criticisms are made in the National Union of Teachers (1980) *Curriculum and Examinations*, being a submission to the House of Commons Select Committee on Education, Science and the Arts, London, NUT; GOLBY, M. (Ed.) (1980) 'Perspectives on the core', *Perspectives*, 2, May; WHITE, J.P. (Ed.) (1981) *No Minister: A Critique of the DES Paper 'The School Curriculum'*, London, University of London Institute of Education.

4   NUT (1980) *op. cit.*; CASTON, G. (1971) 'The Schools Council in context', *Journal of Curriculum Studies*, 3, 1, May.

5   LAWTON, D., (1980) *The Politics of the School Curriculum*, London, Routledge and Kegan Paul, 1980.

6   Different usages of the term 'core curriculum' are considered in MORGAN, C. (1980) 'The common core curriculum: the key issue for government', *Educational Researcher*, 22, 3, June, pp. 182–7, La Trobe University Centre for the Study of Innovation in Education (1981) *Core Curriculum and Values Education: A Literature Review*, Canberra, Curriculum Development Centre; SKILBECK, M. (1982) *op. cit.*, and CRITTENDEN, B. (1982) *Cultural Pluralism and the Common Curriculum*, Melbourne, Melbourne University Press.

7   THE SCHOOLS COUNCIL (1981) *The Practical Curriculum*, London, The Schools Council.

8   CURRICULUM DEVELOPMENT CENTRE, (1980) *A Core Curriculum for Australian Schools*, Canberra, Curriculum Development Centre.

9   HIRST, P.H. (1972) 'Liberal education and the nature of knowldge' in DEARDEN, R.F., HIRST, P.H. and PETERS, R.S. (Eds) *Education and Reason*, London, Routledge and Kegan Paul; PHENIX, P.H. (1964) *Realms of Meanings*, New York, McGraw Hill, CASSIRER, E (1953–57) *The Philosophy of Symbolic Forms*, 3 vols. New Haven, Conn., Yale University Press.

10 DEWEY, J. (1916) *Democracy and Education*, New York, Macmillan, 1916, p. 214.

11 Her Majesty's Inspectorate (1980) *op. cit.* Yet in their criticism of both primary and secondary schooling the Inspectorate frequently object to teaching that seems to be based on transmission theories.

12 Examples are to be found in England, in the writings of Basil Bernstein and Michael White, and in the USA of Michael Apple and Henry Giroux.

13 BALOGH, J. (1982) *Profile Reports for School Leavers*, York. Longmans Resource Unit for Schools Council; GOACHER, B. (1983) *Recording Achievements at 16+*, York, Longmans Resource Unit for Schools Council.

14 In SHAW, G.B. (1889) (Ed.), *Fabian Essays in Socialism*, London, The Fabian Society.

15 Reference here is to the cooperative work following on *Curriculum 11–16* and *Curriculum 11–16: A Review of Progress*.

16 ELLIOT, G., (1980–83) *Self-Evaluation and the Teacher: An Annotated Bibliography and Report on Current Practice, Parts 1–4*, London and Hull, Schools Council/University of Hull.

17 SKILBECK, M., (1983) 'A way out of linger and lurch policies', *Times Educational Supplement*, 3 June.

Education and Social Class: The Curriculum: Discussion

Improvements in the education system have succeeded only in 'jacking up' the whole system whilst failing to reduce the differentials between the advantaged and the disadvantaged groups within it. Thus, the main aim of any curriculum model aware of these inbuilt educational differences between social classes must be to find a means of reducing those differences. How, though, to develop such a model?

One curious feature of current literature dealing with the comprehensive curriculum is the remarkable degree of unanimity in the analyses of present practices and the diagnoses of existing ills. The problems arise when attempting some kind of cure. A clear starting point is needed for a framework for the new curriculum.

David Hargreaves has proposed the twin pillars of the creative/performing arts and a community perspective. This may well prove to be an appropriate model. But we need to begin at an earlier stage.

Our present practice is afflicted by six major rigidities which inhibit or obstruct progressive change or development. There are others, such as the demands imposed by higher education and the restrictions of finance, but the following six are particularly important and symbolic:

1 The rigidity of chronology

We are locked not only into a system, but in a habit of thought which presupposes that learning must take place in groups of a closely similar age. Outside the school system, this is not equally axiomatic.

2 The rigidity of teacher-and-group

Similarly, we have the concept that almost the only learning arrangement is that of the group with the single teacher. As our understanding of the learning process has developed, so this mode has become less appropriate for many learning needs.

3   The rigidity of the primacy of content

As information has become an increasingly necessary social commodity, so the education system has responded by laying increasing stress on curriculum content. A desperate but unavailing struggle has taken place to keep pace with the information explosion in the world at large. We would be better occupied concentrating our efforts on teaching and learning about process rather than content, about convertibility rather than specialization.

4   The rigidity of norm-referenced assessment

Our assessment system has lost contact with the interested parties it has sought to serve. A key factor in this failure is its norm-referenced base which has ensured misconceptions based on ignorance. A criterion-referenced system would better fulfil most of the intended functions of assessment, and in particular its role as an agent of feedback and as a means of monitoring progress.

5   The rigidity of the end-product model

Both our schooling and assessment systems are based on the concept that there is one fixed point at which significant measurement should take place. Any other testing or evaluation should be seen merely as a stage towards that end-product. The notion of the module, the graded test, or the packaged short course with its own built-in assessment — although evident in other systems — is regarded as alien to our own. Those pupils who opt out of subjects, of courses and even of school itself are perceived as having achieved nothing at all in school.

6   The rigidity of lines on the timetable

However we try to disguise it, learning activities in most schools are timetabled into small segments in a fixed pattern, rotating from day to day. This contrasts with the experience of both teachers and pupils in non-school time, when a priority task may dominate a whole day or more, and with the later working pattern for many pupils.

Additionally we need to take account of the limitations imposed by available resources; the resistance of many teachers to proposed changes because of insecurity through cutbacks and threatened jobs and the narrowing of many teachers' professional training; and the increased independence of pupils, less willing to accept direction, more capable of operating alone, and more likely to boycott whatever is regarded as irrelevant.

Thus the pupils themselves are one starting point for what we do in school and we must seek to make better use of the concepts and perspectives which they carry with them before teaching in school begins. This is now clearly recognized in matters of language. But it also has to be acknowledged that pupils often bring with them a greater degree of technological sophistication — through television, computers, video and so on — which has left many teachers untouched. But those same teachers must be another starting point. Without their involvement, change cannot succeed. Once their commitment is underway, parents and other members of the community must be quickly involved as well.

The Nature of Change

We are concerned here then with changing not only the curriculum itself, but also the value system on which it is based, and the aims and objectives towards which it claims to operate. Implicit in what has already been said is the political perspective, suggesting that we are ultimately talking about ways of enabling communities to take control of their own lives and environment — in effect, fundamental social change. The scale of such change might intimidate us and persuade us the task is not worth attempting, but — as Peter Mortimore argues — we should not be deterred by the magnitude of that task.

Opportunities and Agents for Change

One response to the depressing catalogue of statistics produced by Peter Mortimore as evidence of the correlation between social class and educational disadvantage is to lay blame for these failings outside the education system and to argue that solutions also lie in a broader context. But this is too facile. Schools do have opportunities to break through and to find ways of compensating rather than merely facilitating progress along the 'relentless escalator' — once on board, you travel to your destination but your position in relation to those around you does not change. Individual schools and local authorities should be able to break through some of the rigidities and to exploit available agents for change. What is required is a strategy which will find a usable path.

Some access points in the six rigidities are more susceptible to attack than others. We need to decide which are most accessible and what are the most suitable agents for change.

For example, the first rigidity of chronology is currently under attack through the community education movement and its greater flexibility is likely to have its effects elsewhere in the organization of the school. It is also threatened by the development of certificates of educational achievement, where graded tests are likely to feature strongly, breaking down at the same time the fifth rigidity of the end-product model.

In fact, the community education movement is a powerful agent for change in relation to several rigidities; not least it opens up exciting possibilities in terms of the timing of activities and breaking down the lines on the timetable. The argument then is straightforward. The opportunities are there, rigidities can be broken down, agents for change do exist, schools can intervene and change.

Creating Conditions for Change

What remains to be explored is the particular strategy which will address itself to the problem of social class and educational disadvantage in curriculum matters. Here the key is redefinition of the term 'success', since the existing working definitions are based on a very limiting scale of values.

If we can assert what Pat Daunt[2] defined as the 'comprehensive principle' — that the education of all pupils is held to be intrinsically of equal value — not merely in our aims and objectives on paper but in our in-school practice; and if, simultaneously, we give more frequent opportunities for success, not necessarily mediated by the teacher, but with pupils making frank and appropriate judgments of their own work; then we will begin to produce a significant shift of emphasis in our work.

But another shift needs to take place at the same time — and bitter experience has recently shown that without this other changes are doomed to failure. The local community, and parents in particular, must be centrally involved. Schools must take parents into their confidence and attempt to make them sympathetically aware both of the harsh facts (about exam results, the shortcomings of the exam system and of the traditional curriculum, the breakdown of the school/employment 'contract', and so on) and of the school's proposals for breaking out of this restrictive mould.

There are risks in this, especially in an area where the school's aims may be directly at odds with the prevailing local ethos. But there are greater, and indeed terminal, risks in any failure to do this.

Without negotiation teachers would undermine, pupils would boycott (as many do now) and parents would resist. So too without additional teacher-time being made available such changes would fail. But LEAs view teacher-time as money. In the present climate it is highly unlikely that LEAs would improve pupil-teacher ratios for the sake of proposals which they might in any case view with suspicion. The only way therefore is for schools to rethink their own priorities within the set framework.

Values and Social Class

The present system does not give adequate encouragement or reward to what have been described[3] as the three Cs — competencies, curiosity, cooperation. We are geared to a different set of prime values. We should therefore broaden the concept of what constitutes achievement or success — without losing our proper delight in what is termed 'excellence'. What is required is a change in attitude.

For example, some real achievements in physics go unrecognized simply because the existing mode of learning and assessment is strictly limited. Practical and oral ways of showing learning are neither tested nor valued. An 'O' level pass is more likely to show that the candidate knows how to write about the subject in a particular form rather than understanding the content itself.

Furthermore, the present skill model gives primacy to the cognitive-intellectual, rating the theoretical measuring of the speed of light more highly than the successful delivery of a reluctant lamb in farmyard reality. But as there are other ways of showing learning, so there are other ways of knowing — as a glance at pupils' activities in the pottery room or drama room will excitingly show. Although the current assessment model specifically encourages a competitive, individualistic spirit a good deal of what happens in the secondary school is concerned with communal activity in a cooperative spirit, especially in the early years before the assessment model takes control through public exams.

Such concerns are directly related to the issue of class, for the prevailing modes of learning and evaluation — and therefore the measures of success and achievement — are predominantly class-related. The sorts of change advocated here will do much to break this grip. With other ways of achieving success more openly recognized, the self-esteem and the self-image of the pupil able to achieve in that other mode will be greatly enhanced. This should also spill over into improved competence in traditional modes and produce a more acceptable, less hierarchical, skill model operating in public consciousness.

Towards a Curriculum Model

We set out to establish a model which would find a means of reducing the differentials between social classes within the system. To this may now be added that experience shows it necessary to concentrate our efforts on assistance to the disadvantaged by (a) changing the value system; and (b) changing our educational practice. We have also questioned the supposed achievement of those whom the existing system recognizes as achievers.

We have established that our curriculum should be negotiated by the school, the pupils, parents and the whole community network. We have also asserted the need for a new set of values — people should be of equal value and their work likewise (despite awkward questions about conformity and non-conformity, and whether the value is intrinsic or extrinsic).

We have also indicated that we will open up new ways of learning — concentrating on process rather than content — and recognize varied ways of knowing.

Thus we begin to establish our axes:

Figure 1: Pre-model 1

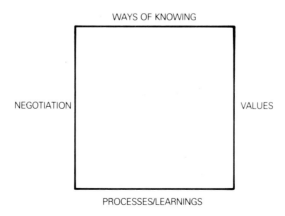

WAYS OF KNOWING

NEGOTIATION

VALUES

PROCESSES/LEARNINGS

Our curriculum will not be without content or outcome: at its centre will be concepts, involving acquired skills, understanding, and other forms of 'knowledge'. The values will probably best feed into the main model rather than forming a part of it. Thus we move to the second stage:

Figure 2: Pre-model 2

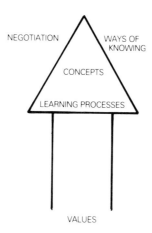

We would look for a constant interaction between the constituent parts, with evaluation renegotiation and renewal taking place, involving the negotiators, who should themselves form the link between the underlying value-system and the curriculum itself:

Figure 3: Pre-model 3

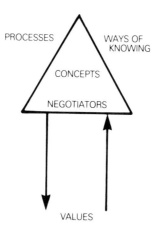

This, however, still appears unsatisfactory. For it is the negotiators who determine the values. Therefore they are outside the main model feeding into it through the values:

Figure 4: Pre-model 4

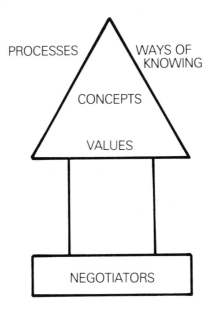

The New Curriculum Model

We are near our final purpose. There is a pleasing balance between the forces involved. But there are other factors still to be included. The way in which the school or the LEA or the secondary system is itself organized has a major part to play as a third active agent (shown as vertical edges) along with the learning processes and the ways of knowing. Our concepts should be more precisely broken down into the *competencies* referred to earlier, the *understanding* which lies deeper than mere knowledge, and the whole area of *feeling* of which we too often tend to fight shy. Thus these three facets of our model become the equally valued outcomes as well as the content — and a more complex and subtle model emerges.

Such a curriculum model might begin to set right the imbalance in the existing system. It would, coincidentally, 'jack up' the whole system too, but not, this time, without seriously reducing the differentials with which we began as our prime target.

Figure 5: The new curriculum model

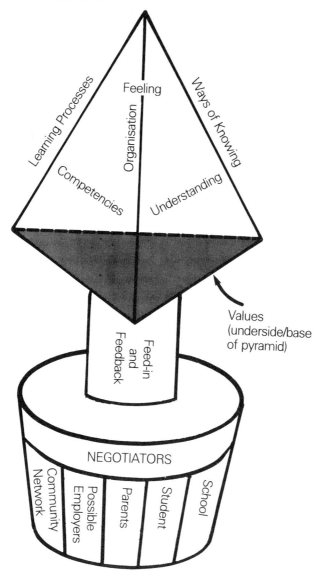

Notes

1 HARGREAVES, D. (1982) *The Challenge for the Comprehensive School*, London, Routledge and Kegan Paul
2 DAUNT, P. *Comprehensive Values*
3 See the MACOS scheme, Jerome Bruner

Towards a Framework for Interpreting Examination Results★

John Gray, David Jesson and Ben Jones

The question why some schools get 'better examination results than others' is important. Much public discussion and evaluation of schools is premised on the not unreasonable assumption that it is schools themselves that are largely responsible for their pupils' performance. Yet a moment's reflection will also suggest that the intake a secondary school receives is also an important determinant of how well its pupils will be doing five years later in the examination room. A realistic assessment of a school's contribution to its pupils' academic development lies, obviously enough, somewhere between these two poles, yet, to date, we have relatively little by way of systematic evidence on this topic. It has been one aim of the SSRC-funded *Contexts Project* to provide a framework for such discussions; the purpose of the present article is to summarize some of the more important points to emerge from our research.

Context for the Research

Schools were required by the 1980 Education Act to publish their examination results and such information was universally inserted in school prospectuses for the first time in 1982. This is probably the most explicit, and certainly the most rough-and-ready, form of account-ability to be introduced to date. Those most suitable forms for the presentation of such information have been a matter for considerable debate, both nationally and within individual LEAs. Underlying such debates has been a genuine concern that 'raw' examination results

★ Reprinted from Sheffield Educational Research, Current Highlights No 5

might be falsely interpreted as indicators of schools' effectiveness. Most educators with whom we have spoken appear to be in agreement that the details demanded by law are potentially misleading.

Despite the fact that examinations feature prominently in the lives of secondary school teachers and their pupils, surprisingly little is known about schools' policies and practices towards them. Her Majesty's Inspectors have contributed more to this discussion than most but even they have dwelt only briefly on the topic. They observed, in their most recent national survey of secondary education, that 'rightly or wrongly, examination results were perceived by the schools as the sole indicators of (their) success in the eyes of the community' (Department of Education and Science, 1979, p. 248–9). Our own discussions to date confirm that the vast majority of schools are interested in obtaining the 'best' results for their pupils. What they mean by this phrase, however, is more problematic.

The unease of educators towards the present examination system was captured by a large survey of experienced practitioners in Sheffield during the mid-seventies. Whilst a considerable majority of those surveyed believed that 'examinations provide (d) a good way by which teachers could evaluate their performance in the classroom' there was a much more even split between those who believed that the existing system provided 'a satisfactory yardstick by which society (could) judge the academic quality of its schools', and those who did not (Wilcox and Garforth, 1976). At the same time, many educators with whom we have discussed this issue have voiced considerable doubts about the wisdom of attributing to examinations the most prominent place amongst their overall objectives.

The reasons for such doubts are not difficult to fathom. Given the strong relationships between a school's intake and the subsequent performance of their pupils, schools are likely to resent being attributed the greater proportion of the responsibility. Broadly speaking, they fear (rightly in our view) that their efforts will be publicly evaluated in direct relation to the quality of their intakes — such a system benefits schools, of course, that are fortunate enough to have more favourable intakes.

Researchers of school effectiveness have long been concerned with the question of how one can most fairly judge the efforts of schools with differing intakes. Two examples of this approach are the study *Fifteen Thousand Hours* by Rutter and others (1979) and the work of Gray, McPherson and Raffe (1983) in Scotland. Building on this work, the question whether we can create a fairer framework for the public evaluation of *all* schools forms a major part of the agenda for the *Contexts Project* (1983–1985, HR8602). The realistic answer, given current resources and procedures, may be negative but the research is committed to exploring, with interested schools and LEAs, what such a system might look like and to identifying the barriers that would need to be overcome for it to be implemented.

A number of interested schools and local authorities have offered to help us with our research, and with their assistance we have explored a variety of issues. Some of the key areas to emerge to date are outlined below.

Which Summary Measures?

Which summary measures of examination results should be employed for the purposes of comparison? We have already encountered a variety of suggestions but there is some agreement that the information that may be usefully gleaned from pass rates (that is the proportions of pupils achieving 'passes' in given subjects) is not particularly helpful. LEAs seem to show some preference for percentages of pupils achieving given levels of attainment or average numbers of 'O' level/CSE grade 1 passes per pupil. We are not sure, as yet, why particular summary measures have been adopted although in some cases an initial desire to compare performances with the old grammar school system has been cited.

Most of the current summary measures of examination results tend to ignore lower levels of attainment, especially CSE performance below grade 1, even though these may represent perfectly respectable or, indeed, exemplary results for the particular pupils concerned. Perhaps the biggest difficulty encountered to date, however, is how one obtains an overall profile of performance that crosses the GCE/CSE boundary. A number of LEAs (and some individual schools) have begun to adopt a scoring system first employed by the Inner London Education Authority, which has pioneered a number of important developments in the area of publishing examination results. In this system a grade A pass at 'O' level is given a score of 7 points, a grade B 6 points, a grade C 5 points, a grade D 4 points, and a grade E 3 points. A CSE grade 1 is treated as equivalent to an 'O' level pass at grade C and awarded 5 points; a grade 2 gets 4 points, a grade 3, 3 points, a grade 4, 2 points and a grade 5, 1 point.

Whilst this approach is an improvement on some other

approaches, the somewhat arbitrary nature of the assumptions under-lying the weighting of the different grades of performance needs to be recognized. We have encountered the view that it does not actually matter which yardstick of examination performance one employs (that they all measure basically the same underlying dimension) but this remains, in our view, to be satisfactorily established. In brief, whilst there is some agreement that the existing and available summary measures of examination results are inadequate for the purposes to which they are being put, there is as yet little agreement about what should be developed.

Predicting Results from Intakes

How far can schools' examination results be predicted from knowledge of their intakes? As a broad generalization, and summarizing the results of a very wide range of studies, the answer is that up to 80 per cent of the differences between schools can be statistically 'explained' by differ-ences in their intakes (Gray, 1981). Because we can 'explain' something in statistical terms, however, does not mean that we actually under-stand in any detail what it is about the backgrounds and characteristics of the pupils that produces particular levels of performance; but, nonetheless, even the most unsophisticated measures of their back-grounds or prior attainments seem to explain very considerable propor-tions of the differences in results.

Two interesting trends have emerged in the data we have explored to date. First, the greater the extent to which available measures of intake are measures of individual pupils, the greater the proportions of the differences in results one can explain. But even rough-and-ready measures of pupils' backgrounds at particular schools, such as percent-ages on free school meals or the social class of the catchment area, enable one to explain around half of the differences in schools' examination results. Measures which are intuitively more satisfactory such as performance at entry on tests of attainment in mathematics, reading or verbal reasoning, enable one to explain upwards of two-thirds of the differences. Second, the more measures one uses in combination, especially those relating to prior attainments, the more one's predictions are improved. These trends have held up across all the schools and LEAs we have studied, although the strength of the relationships observed has differed from authority to authority.

The School's Contribution

How large are the differences potentially attributable to schools them-selves? Our overall conclusion is that they are considerably smaller than the sorts of figures that are usually bandied around in public debates. This may best be illustrated by reference to the performance of schools serving socially disadvantaged areas, in which we have been particular-ly interested.

Take Southtown, for example, one of the local authorities whose results we have looked at in greater detail. Amongst the most disadvan-taged quarter of schools as regards intake, the median school averaged 1.6 'O' level/CSE grade 1 passes per pupil. At one of these schools, however, the pupils averaged 2.2 passes each whilst at another school in the same group they averaged only 0.8 passes. The most and least *effective* of the schools amongst this disadvantaged group of schools differed, then, by an average of 1.4 passes per pupil; but, of course, the remaining schools in this group differed by much less. We found similar differences amongst the other three groups of schools when they were ranked according to the extent of social advantage/disadvan-tage in their catchment areas. The overall levels of examination performance in Northtown, on the other hand, were somewhat lower than in Southtown. Indeed, in the most disadvantaged quarter of schools in this LEA the median performance for the group was only 0.9 'O' level/CSE grade 1 passes per pupil. We say 'only' advisedly because, just as the overall performance levels of an individual school depend in large measure on its social and intellectual make-up, so do those of an LEA. What is interesting here, however, is that within this most disadvantaged quarter of schools the range of differences between the most and least effective schools was considerably smaller than in Southtown, amounting to 0.8 passes per pupil; again, the remaining schools in this group differed by less.

These findings ignore levels of achievement below CSE grade 1. The Inner London Education Authority's analyses provide some more inclusive information. Within the most disadvantaged fifth of their schools, the median school obtained an average of 7 points per pupil on the ILEA scale mentioned earlier; this was equivalent to two CSE grade 3s and a CSE grade 5 per pupil. The least effective school in this group achieved 4 points and the most effective 11 points. What marked out an 'outstanding' school from the rest amongst this group of schools then amounted to a little more than the equivalent of a CSE grade 3 pass per pupil. These estimates should be compared with the differences amongst the most advantaged fifth of schools where the median score was some seven 'O' level/CSE grade 1 passes per pupil; amongst this group of schools pupils at the 'outstanding' ones achieved nine passes each, or two more than one would have predicted from knowledge of their intake.

Comparing the one group of schools (that is the most disadvantaged) with the other, (that is the most advantaged) therefore, what seems to distinguish 'excellence' in one case is the equivalent of a CSE grade 3 pass per pupil whereas in the other it is two 'O' levels. We would argue that a system for evaluating examination results which wanted to be equally fair to all schools, regardless of their intakes, would need to value the two achievements in equal measure.

What Makes a Difference?

Even allowing for differences in intakes, some schools still appear to get better examination results than others. As yet we do not know why. However, a considerable number of plausible hypotheses are available for investigation. These include the fact that schools differ in the extent to which they are 'exam-oriented'. One school, for example, may routinely enter pupils for seven subjects whilst another enters them for eight. Such decisions are usually justified on educational grounds but how one decides that one strategy or the other is preferable is obviously a matter of judgment.

Schools also differ in their actual examination entry policies. They may enter different proportions of their cohorts in general for examinations; they may make selective use of examination boards; they may use dual entry strategies for GCE and CSE; and they may regard different 'pass rates' as satisfactory indicators of their 'success'.

Some exploratory work which we have undertaken on the results of two 'social priority' schools (Gray and Nicholl, 1982) suggests that the strategies outlined above may explain up to half the differences observed in overall levels of examination performance between schools with largely comparable intakes.

One other important area is also suggested by our preliminary work. As Rutter *et al* (1979) have argued, schools may differ in 'ethos', some creating circumstances and atmospheres which are more conducive to pupils making academic progress than others. And finally, some schools and teachers may well be more effective in teaching or preparing their pupils for public examinations. One can only assert this with confidence, however, when one has taken the other factors outlined in this article into account.

The Need for Other Outcomes

Because examination results are readily available and tell one some important things about a school it is easy to forget that education has wider aims and objectives. Many aspects of education do not lend themselves to easy measurement but are no less important for that. Furthermore, we believe it is still an open question whether schools which get 'good' examination results, given their intakes, achieve equally good results in other areas as well. Our view is based, in part, on the conflicting research evidence (Rutter *et al*, 1979; Gray, McPherson and Raffe, 1983) but also on the absence to date of sufficient data to make wholly satisfactory judgments. We still think it is likely that success in the examination room is bought at a price and we should like to know more about what that might involve. But, until both individual schools and local authorities collect data on a wider range of outcomes than at present, there is a danger that the public will continue to believe that schools should be judged merely by their examination results.

References

DEPARTMENT OF EDUCATION AND SCIENCE (1979) *Aspects of Secondary Education: A Survey by HM Inspectors of Schools*, London, HMSO.

GRAY, J. (1981) 'A competitive edge: Examination results and the probable limits of secondary school effectiveness', *Educational Review*, 33, 1, pp. 25–35.

GRAY, J., McPHERSON, A.F., and RAFFE, D. (1983) *Reconstructions of Secondary Education Theory: Myth and Practice Since the War*, London, Routledge and Kegan Paul.

GRAY, J. and NICHOLL, A. (1982) 'Comparing examination results in two social priority schools: four plausible hypotheses', *School Organization*, 2, 3, pp. 255–72.

RUTTER, M., MAUGHAN, B., MORTIMORE, P. and OUSTON, J. (1979) *Fifteen Thousand Hours: Secondary Schools and Their Effects on Children*, London, Open Books.

WILCOX, B. and GARFORTH, J. (1976) 'Attitudes towards examinations', *The Secondary Survey, Report No. 1*, Education Department, Sheffield MDC.

Education and Social Class: Examinations: Discussion

Success in examinations heralds expectations and aspirations and provides access to status and positions of power and influence in society.

If education is about reinforcing an acceptance of one's position in society then any change in the means of control or in the organization of schools would be untenable. If, however education is concerned with developing individuals and capitalizing on their talents and potential, then the system must change in order to reduce the waste in human talent and to create greater fairness in the distribution of life chances.

Peter Mortimore highlights the class differentials which still exist in schools and are perpetuated by the continual dominance of examinations as the tool for measuring success and failure. Exams measure specific skills and by their very nature discriminate against a large section of the population.

Mortimore illustrates that pupil progress in school is clearly related to the social class of the parent. For example, the highest proportion of children aged 7 with poor reading and arithmetic scores and in need of special educational provision were from social class 5 (NCDS, 1972). Similarly, of pupils gaining five high grades in public examinations, 39 per cent were from non-manual parents compared with 12 per cent from manual parents. UCCA records also reveal considerable class differences. Farrant (1981) points out that between 1962 and 1977 the proportion of the age group going on to higher education rose from 7.5 per cent to 13 per cent. But most of the increase was taken up by the middle classes.

Philip Venning (1983) also uses Farrant and UCCA statistics to show that the decline in the proportion of working-class students attending university will have 'crucial implications for future numbers in higher education'. He cites the shortfall as about one third from working-class homes and believes that the 'coincidence of this fall with the extension of comprehensive reorganization and the elimination of grammar schools is too striking for the political implications to be ignored'. He suggests that the evidence is such that 'no-one can say categorically that comprehensives are, or are not to blame'. However, while there has been a decline in the number of working-class children attending university, numbers to polytechnics and the Open University have increased.

Underlying the purpose of exams is the notion of selection. What, in fact, has occurred is the selection process being delayed from 11 to 16. The implications of this are only too well-known to teachers in secondary schools. The exam system forms a stranglehold on the curriculum.

Should schools be in the business of selecting children for what is going to happen to them after they leave? Employers assume that children will have been tested and assessed. Should this assessment be made by employers rather than schools — as is already happening in some of the larger industries?

Desmond Nuttall (1983) claims that exams are used to 'pick out the most promising applicants for jobs or for particular forms of education'. Sometimes the best few are selected 'irrespective of the absolute standard of performance'. On other occasions 'the examination is used to set the minimum acceptable performance level ... more akin to a process of attesting minimum competency'. Nuttall reveals that research statistics indicate that although universities and employers use a variety of criteria for selection, exam results are a crucial factor, not least in the process of shortlisting. He challenges the validity of using such information as a predictor for future success and offers statistics to refute any significant correlation between exam results and future success.

He suggests open access to higher education on a first come first served basis. In 1982 over 50 per cent of Open University students with no formal qualification higher than CSE were successful, whereas nearly a quarter of those with 'A' levels were unsuccessful. If exams are such poor predictors for future success, why do we still set such store by them?

Recent legislation in the 1980 Education Act has made it mandatory for schools to publish their exam results, thus introducing a form of accountability which measures only one aspect of a school's work. Gray and Jones (1983) cite the HMI national survey 1979:

> ... rightly or wrongly, examination results were perceived by the schools as the sole indicators of (their) success in the eyes of the community.

If exams become the yardstick by which schools are compared and judged by society, then the presentation of raw data needs exploration. Gray and Jones in an investigation of school effectiveness argue that the intake the school receives is crucial in any comparison between schools. Summarizing results of wide-ranging studies, they suggest that 'up to 80 per cent of differences between schools can be explained by differences in intake'.

Mortimore (1983) maintains that 'the more effective schools do not actually alter the social class pattern of achievements, but rather they appear to jack up the attainment of *all* pupils without closing the gap between the classes'. This has implications for those working in schools and begs the question as to the appropriateness of a yardstick which measures specific and easily measurable skills in an arena which is concerned with a plethora of activity and a variety of aims and goals. In short, the system has changed but the yardstick has not.

Although exams do measure relatively objective aspects of what goes on in schools, there are many aspects of education no less important which do not lend themselves to easy measurement. It may well be necessary to reconsider what is meant by ability and by what yardstick competence can be satisfactorily assessed.

One remains aware of Venning's implied criticism of comprehensive schools. Would the removal of exams militate against the mobility of the working-class children and the introduction of a different yardstick become yet another implement for the middle classes to manipulate and make their own?

Challenging children is an important part of education but the nature and context of assessments are also crucial. Exams test memory and regurgitation of information within time constraints with the emphasis heavily on written skills and abstract concepts. Altering the definition of ability can shift the focus to an active and practical approach to problem-solving with a value on oral skills and communication through other creative media such as video and tapes.

To do this suggests a fundamental change in the nature of school and a reform of the exam system where the process is as important as the product and where measurement of what children can do rather than what they cannot is emphasized.

Like all innovation in education, such a process will be slow and to be successful there should be a multi-faceted approach. For example, the new Secondary Examinations Council could put pressure on the universities; there could be a central government initiative; links with industry could be improved. A new programme of in-service training could be developed with practising teachers and colleges of higher education, together with a major public relations exercise to inform parents, councillors and others in the community. Perhaps, though, the most effective catalyst for change would be active consideration of a new model of education designed to break down existing barriers.

One essential part of this new model must be the introduction of pupil profiling. Despite the complexity of profiling they could well eventually replace the exam system — see the Oxford Certificate of Educational Achievement. In addition, once the mechanics and detail of profiling have been mastered and simplified, they could be the source of a great deal of information, replacing some of the more tedious and time-consuming administrative tasks which teachers have to do such as reports, feedback to children, parents' evening, listing and categorizing achievements including extra-curricular activities.

Several pilot schemes are operating in the country and some underlying principles are emerging. These include incorporating graded assessments as part of a formative diagnostic process which would make explicit the achievements of pupils. A dialogue should be established between teachers and pupils with the pupils becoming involved in self-evaluation and negotiated assessment. This would create an increase in the dignity within the teacher/pupil relationship which can result in the pupil, explicitly and implicitly, assessing teacher competence. Only positive aspects of pupils should be reflected in the summative document. At present all pupils have a school file and this could form the basis of a profile so long as issues of confidentiality between pupil and teacher and pupil and parent can be overcome.

With such breaking down of barriers in school come a shift in the nature of school and a change in the role of the teacher. The teacher would cease to be the expert and the transmitter of knowledge and would become the interpreter and facilitator. More time would be needed to complete profiles leading to more flexible working arrangements in school with an emphasis on relevance and individual needs (see the Coventry Project). Schools could become a valuable resource within the community and a place where other members of the community would be welcome.

By providing for local and individual needs, would this continue to have a detrimental effect on working-class children and inhibit their mobility still further? To ensure that children of aspiring and concerned parents should not have their life chances jeopardized, the profile must have credibility and contain positive and as far as possible impartial statements.

If this form of assessment were to gain wide currency, with selection at 16 taken out of the control of schools, the implications for the curriculum would be dramatic. There would be an increase in individualized learning schemes. Modular courses could be introduced providing motivation and relevance operating on a similar principle to the Open University system. With the introduction of new technology courses and government intervention with TVEI — which may provide extra impetus for change — young people could make more decisions for themselves, an ability the traditional exam system restricts.

Given that the school is central in the community and adults other than teachers become an important resource, education should not be seen as an activity that ends at the age of 16. Points of access to further and higher education should never be closed because of age. Access courses providing catch-up points, such as City and Guilds and pre-vocational courses, should be available to all.

Education is concerned with preparing children for life in a society where people need to adapt to new problems and take responsibility for their own actions. It is essential that young people are encouraged to utilize their potential rather than waste their talents. By removing young people from the 'arena of failure' new generations of children can develop positive attitudes towards learning, leading to an acceptance of schools and teachers as valuable resources, enabling them to negotiate their own ways of acquiring knowledge and adapting it for their own purposes.

References

FARRANT, J. (1981) 'Trends in admissions' in FULTON, O. (Ed.) *Access to Higher Education*, Guildford, SRHE.

GRAY, J. and JONES, B. 'Towards a framework for interpreting examination results' *Current Highlights No 5*, Sheffield Educational Research (in this volume).

Mortimore, P. and J. (1983) *Education and Social Class*, PRISE conference, Cambridge.

Nuttall, D. (1983) 'Unnatural selection', *Times Educational Supplement*, 18 November.

Venning, P. (1983) 'The mystery of the vanishing students', *Times Educational Supplement*, 25 November.

Privatization of Education

Richard Pring

Introduction

Embodied in Butler's Education Act of 1944 was a policy of secondary education for all, not just for those who can personally afford it. Education was to be provided according to age, aptitude and ability rather than according to private means. It is this policy, pursued by successive administrations since the war, which is now being reversed by a policy of privatization.

The seriousness of this reversal of policy is exacerbated by the slow, quiet way in which it is being achieved. Indeed, it is privatization by stealth. No-one has declared that the education service should be privatized but there is increasing evidence to show that this is what is happening and furthermore that it is the result of deliberate policy.

There are different ways in which education might be said to be privatized and these are explained in other sections of this chapter. Indeed, my main aim is to map this rather complex territory and to show the many, often unnoticed, ways in which the educational system is becoming privatized. But in general privatization means making the provision and the quality of education increasingly dependent on private means. There are, however, different ways in which this is achieved. First, it is achieved through making services, that should be free within the maintained sector, dependent upon parents paying for them. Secondly, it is achieved through encouraging and enabling people to shift their support from the maintained sector to private schools.

The ways of privatizing in the second sense are, broadly speaking, two: first, there is public, especially financial, support for private institutions as part of a policy of making them more accessible to people who otherwise would use the maintained sector; secondly, there is an impoverishment of the maintained sector of education such that parents are driven, often against their own wishes, into choosing heavily subsidized private education. But whichever aspect of privatization one is considering — whether in the sense of having to purchase at *private expense* services within the *public system* or whether in the sense of supporting at *public expense* educational services in *private institutions* — the result is the same: viz., a deliberate shifting of responsibility from the community to private institutions and thus the gradual erosion of a commitment to a common education service to *all* young people on the basis of equal opportunity.

Such a development has its attractions for certain groups of people. It claims to bring to education the *apparent* advantages of the market economy, namely, responsiveness (through increased 'parental choice') to consumer pressure which (it is said) would raise standards and ensure the provision of what people want. The best known 'market economy' approach is the voucher system which until recently was being considered by the Secretary of State for Education and Science. This system has been tested by the Kent Education Authority but was abandoned after a two year trial because it was too costly and disruptive in maintaining mobile classrooms and teachers and because of its deleterious effect on unpopular schools. But there are many less obvious ways in which education is becoming privatized, in line with a more general philosophy of how social services should be run and individual people provided for.

Privatization is encouraged, however, not simply because of the claimed *practical* advantages of the market place but also because of its virtues. And this indeed reflects a most important shift in the moral climate within which private education is now considered. It is illustrated in an address to an 'old boys' gathering by the former Secretary of State for Education and Science, Mr. Mark Carlisle, where he argued that parents who can afford to buy an education for their children should make it their duty to do so and not be beholden to the state for their schooling. He said:

> I am old fashioned enough to believe that not only is it one's own responsibility rather than that of the state to provide for one's own family, but that, if one is fortunate enough to be able to afford to do so, it is one's right and duty.

The significance of what I see to be a change in the moral climate lies not in the establishment of the *right* of parents to purchase education privately, for that is already well established. The significance lies rather in the popular basis it provides for supporting with public funds a private system which, in its selection of pupils and in the conduct of its affairs, is not accountable to the larger community despite the profound effect it has upon that community. As Colin McCabe said in a talk on comprehensive schools:

> It is of course no surprise that the Tory party is commited to a private education system which does so much to perpetuate and reproduce our ruling elite in all its ignorant and inefficient isolation. *What is surprising is that the Tory party can now assume that the defence of public schools is a vote winner for large sections of the electorate.*

It is this moral claim, as well as the ones of practical advantage, that need to be challenged. 'Market economy' is not only a dangerously misleading analogy for understanding educational processes. It does not provide the ethical base for how we, as a community, should assume responsibility for the education of young people. *All* children matter and have a right to the cultural and material advantages that education can bring, not just those whose parents have learnt to play the market effectively. But the improvement of schools for *everyone* is a slow and uphill task that requires resources, community backing, and long-term planning, not the short-term pressures arising out of market forces.

What then in detail are the objections to privatization?

Reasons against Privatization

Less Accountability

Increasing privatization means decreasing accountability of the education service since so many important decisions affecting children and society will be taken outside the normal democratically agreed safeguards that presently operate. Education is thus *treated* as a private matter. However, it is not a private matter. How society educates its young is of immense public importance, especially in the private sector where so many leading and influential public figures are educated. And all parts of the service, therefore, need to be made properly accountable.

As the private sector becomes increasingly dependent on public funds the lack of accountabilty and public control becomes increasingly anomalous. The possible consequence of this increasing dependence on public subsidies is of course something that the private sector is becoming aware of as is illustrated in a paper by Tim Devlin, then Director of the Independent Schools Information Service (ISIS) who, because of this increased indebtedness, argues for closer partnership with the maintained sector.

Less Resources

I estimate that the private sector is subsidized by something between £200m and £300m per year. Considerable resources given to a privileged few are thus taken away from the less privileged many.

Undermining of Comprehensive Education

The comprehensive school aims to make available a broad, relevant (and therefore practical) curriculum. This requires providing access *for all children* to (i) the tools of intellectual discourse and criticism so often associated with the grammar school; and (ii) the practical abilities of the craftsman and the technician. Privatization, however, cannot be disconnected from a two-tier system of education — the more academic, prestigious and less practical being preserved in the privatized sector for children whose parents know where educational advantage lies; the more practically relevant, vocationally-oriented and skills-based education being advocated for the public sector. Those educated in the public sector and those educated in the private sector will all equally suffer from the impoverishment of the comprehensive ideal. And indeed we should watch with interest the impact of the MSC inspired Technical and Vocational Education Initiative (TVEI) upon such developments. Accepted with enthusiasm by many within the maintained system, it is a far cry from the mainstream curriculum of private schools, and there is a danger that this (a more practical, technically oriented curriculum geared to further education) might be seen as the 'relevant' programme for largely working class pupils, whilst the rest pursue a traditionally academic curriculum in the subsidized private sector.

Socially and Economically Divisive

Privatization entails an enlarged public/private divide, and with it a set of attitudes about *groups* of people that is socially divisive. This is apparent to anyone who talks to pupils from private schools about children in the local comprehensive, and vice versa.

Removal of Influential People

An impoverished public sector drives more people, often unwillingly, into the private. Less people remain who have the influence and ability to ensure that schools are properly resourced and staffed. Parental choice, exercised successfully by some, leaves behind an increasing proportion of the disadvantaged (not knowing how to choose freely) and of the disgruntled (unable to exercise that choice). As Sir Fred Clarke argued:

> We can hardly continue ... to contemplate an England where the mass of the people coming on by one educational path are to be governed for the most part by a minority advancing by a quite separate and more favoured path.

Curtailment of Choice

For the majority of people who are unable to take advantage of the subsidized private sector — either they have not the means or their choices are not accepted — the maintained sector, deprived of resources, is able to provide fewer services, not more, and thus less parental choice.

Lower Morale and Efficiency in the Maintained Sector

Teachers increasingly find their work difficult in a school where vital resources depend upon private sources (unavailable in poorer areas), where energies are devoted to fund-raising rather than to teaching, and where (through lack of resources) aspiring parents find it necessary to send their children to private schools, assisted in their task by public funds.

But the general policy of privatization must not be confused with particular aspects of it — with, say, the voucher system or Assisted Places Scheme. And it is the purpose of this chapter to show the different ways in which it is taking place. These might be divided into two categories which, respectively, provide the headings for the next two sections:

(i)   privatization in the sense of purchasing at private expense services within the maintained sector;
(ii) privatization in the sense of enabling and encouraging people to have their children educated privately rather than in the maintained sector.

Privatization in the Sense of Making Public Education Increasingly Dependent on Private Means

This dependence on private means for an adequate educational service is one of the most worrying features of what is happening to schools and colleges. It is worrying for two reasons. First, it leaves large numbers of young people, whose parents have not the private means to pay, severely disadvantaged. Secondly, it is undermining the principle, almost universally accepted until recently, that *all* children have a right to an education according to age, aptitude and ability rather than according to parental means. And yet headteachers are put into a difficult, 'no win' situation. Either they seek private sources of funding for their school (thereby undermining the principle of free education for all) or they allow the resources of the school to become insufficient for maintaining satisfactory educational performance. It is estimated for example, as a result of an NUT survey, that in 1981 at least £500,000 was raised by parent teachers associations in Surrey, much of which was spent on basic resources. The local branch of CASE (Campaign for the Advancement of State Education) in Merton estimate that £2–3000 per year is raised in each secondary school to help pay for essentials such as pencils, art materials, books and paper. Weymouth Grammar School has raised, through parental covenants, £10,000 to help pay wages of laboratory assistants, and school secretaries to restore a cut in their working hours imposed by Dorset County Council. Six years of parental covenanting at Hemel Hempstead Comprehensive School, Hertfordshire, now provides half the running costs of the school, the whole of which would normally be regarded as the responsibility of the authority. As David Grant, the Head, declared:

We are not really a maintained school. Most weekends, parents come in to help redecorate and repair the building. It would fall down around us if they did not.

Presently the school is aiming to build from such privately provided funds a technology centre so that more children can take 'O' level technology. At two schools at Sutton in Surrey parental contributions exceeded the amount for running costs provided by the local education authority.

These are a few examples of how a school comes to rely on private sources for providing an essential public service. And the resort to covenanting will become increasingly popular. But one should remain under no illusion as to what is happening — an abrogation of the principle that all children are entitled to free secondary education.

It is important, however, to see the different ways in which private means are subsidizing public education. For this purpose certain distinctions need to be made.

Lessons

Certain school activities, normally part of the curriculum, are increasingly regarded as extras for which payment has to be made — in particular, swimming and music. For example, partly as a result of poor response from parents, who were asked for voluntary donations, the Education Committee of Hereford and Worcester LEA first proposed to scrap music tuition and subsequently suggested a private trust to organize tuition (to which the LEA would contribute). Parents would pay but would be able, because the trust was to be charitable, to covenant their fees. Or, again, private instrumental music teachers in Surrey were practising in maintained schools in school time using school facilities. Despite the dubious legality of the development, it was a matter of either private tuition or of no tuition at all. Similarly Solihull were charging for swimming lessons and transport to and from the baths which could add up to £1 per child. But this was in violation of Section 61(1) of the 1944 Education Act according to which no fees shall be charged in respect of admission to any school maintained by an LEA or in respect of the education provided in any such school. Where however, does the charging for lessons stop? In one local authority, where there was an estimated four-fifths reduction in remedial work in primary schools, wealthier parents were obtaining outside help during school hours at the rate of £10 per hour.

Books and Teaching Materials

It is clear from the HMI reports on expenditure policies within LEAs that the real value of spending on capitation has fallen considerably in some authorities, and that in many cases parent-teacher associations (PTAs) are being asked to pay for what previously were regarded as essentials. But the line between essential and non-essentials is obviously blurred — making this aspect of privatization all the more difficult to measure. Is, for example, the payment by parents for computers within the school, as a condition for having computer appreciation courses, an example of the increasing privatization of the public sector? It is interesting to note that in figures provided by the Educational Publishers Council on per capita spending on books, the figures for Somerset *included* the money raised for this purpose by parents. Difficulties arise, too, in the case of replacing essential equipment that is expensive. The following are examples of how privatization is taking place:

(i)   Department of Industry financed computers to LEA schools on a 50:50 basis, but one authority insisted that the parents find the 50 per cent and running costs.

(ii)   Esher Sixth-Form college launched a £20,000 appeal to raise money for computers and library books.

(iii) Parents of Churchill School, Avon, pledged to covenant £60,000 in four years to a charitable trust for spending on such 'extras' as library and text books and on scientific and laboratory equipment.

All these are in addition to the examples cited in the opening paragraph of this section. But there are, of course, many examples that parents and governors of schools could give. There is a danger that, as the educational budget is cut, so will there arise the *expectation* that essential resources should depend upon private fund-raising.

School Maintenance

This has been an easy target for savings. It is increasingly assumed that PTA funds might be used or, where materials are provided by the LEA, voluntary labour from parents and teachers employed to do the job. For example, Surrey County Council supplies painting and decorating materials if the school can supply voluntary labour, and Gloucestershire too will provide public money to parents for materials if they agree to decorate the school. Such a policy will, however, result in different standards for different schools. Poorer areas will suffer more from cuts since parents are more likely to lack the money and motivation.

Youth Allowance

The Youth Training Scheme (YTS), financed by the Manpower Services Commission, guarantees a year's scheme of training with at least thirteen weeks off-the-job education and training. Each trainee will receive a minimum of £26 weekly allowance. Such an allowance is denied to those of their age group who remain at school in full-time education. By contrast with the trainees, those who remain on in school are being penalized financially. The effect of this upon the maintained sector of education is incalculable. Full-time education will be increasingly limited to those whose families can afford to forego the £26 per week that otherwise would supplement the family income. Many young people will take training courses in private institutions rather than continue with their education, not because the training suits their abilities and interests, but because they cannot afford to do otherwise.

Miscellaneous

There are many other ways in which educational services indirectly depend upon private means: clothing for sporting and other activities; school uniforms; (the basic cost of uniform in secondary education is over £40); school outings and trips; and transport to and from school. It is important to enquire into the extent to which children are debarred from certain curriculum activities because they have not the money for clothing, equipment, or travel. It is interesting to note, for example, how increasingly the cost of entry to examinations is being borne by parents and how authorities such as Cumbria and Oxfordshire have withdrawn financial support for travel expenses incurred in attending interviews for places in higher education, which at a time of increasing competition must limit severely the opportunities for children in poor financial circumstances.

Privatization in the Sense of Enabling and Encouraging Parents to have their Children Educated Privately

Privatization in this sense is achieved in two ways: first, by subsidization of the private sector; secondly, by impoverishing the public or maintained sector.

Subsidization of the Private Sector

The extent to which this is occurring is not as widely recognized as it should be. Certainly it is reaching the stage where one could question the right of many private schools to remain independent, that is, not accountable to the wider public for the basis on which they select pupils and on which they organize their curriculum. The two main ways in which these subsidies are provided (though there are several others) are first, by direct payment of fees from public funds and secondly, (indirectly) through tax concessions.

Direct payment

(i) *Assisted place scheme*

This scheme, by which the government pays the fees at independent schools of the more able children, is currently providing 14,000 places at a cost to the taxpayer of £10m. It is, however, a scheme that will expand considerably and, by 1987, when it will have provided places for several years of entry into private education, it will be costing about £50m per year. The government, however, is thinking about an extension of the scheme and it has been suggested by Peter Brooke, Parliamentary Under-Secretary at the DES, that it could provide education opportunities for children from problem families, children with handicaps such as dyslexia, and children in need of boarding education.

There are some reservations amongst those within the private sector. The Director of ISIS forsees that in future the main attack on private schools will be focussed on the public subsidies, since they blurr the distinction between 'public' and 'private' thereby providing a threat to the independence of the private sector. For those reasons John Rae, Headmaster of Westminster School, warns the independent schools against participating in the scheme, and argues that the private sector should take public money only for services where these cannot be offered within the maintained sector. Indeed, the subsidization of the private sector has prompted the proposal from the Headmaster of Marlborough for a new hybrid institution called a joint-stock school, a partial privatization of certain maintained schools by *joint* funding from parents and local authorities. Parents would pay for the bulk of the equipment and maintenance whilst the authority would have responsibility for salaries and school property. As the Headmaster of Marlborough explained, it would be a matter of tapping the trickle of parental contributions to state schools and of turning them into a flood by finding 'fresh ways of spreading independence'.

(ii)   *Fees for HM forces and government personnel*

Public money is fed directly into private schools by other ways, too. According to the ISIS *Annual Census 1983*, nearly 17,000 pupils at independent schools are receiving contribution to fees from local education authorities. A further 13,000 pupils have parents in HM forces and, in most cases, their fees will be paid out of public funds. A further 15,000 have parents overseas, most of whom will be working for government or for multi-national companies who will pay their fees.

(iii)   *Fees for children with special needs*

Many of the places purchased by the LEA are for pupils with special needs which the maintained sector cannot meet, for example:

(a)   maladjusted or physically or mentally handicapped children;
(b)   pupils who are musically, etc, very gifted;
(c)   pupils with social needs.

Category (a) might increase considerably upon the implementation of the 1981 Education Act when it is found that there are not enough places within the maintained sector to enable an authority to meet its responsibilities. The 1981 Act includes approval of independent schools for taking handicapped pupils. On the other hand, it should be emphasized that some local authorities are seeking to reduce expenditure on private education on this particular group of pupils. Devon, for instance, is reducing its bill of over £500,000 on fees to the private sector by opening its own school for maladjusted children.

(iv)   *Youth training scheme*

The Youth Training Scheme (YTS) under the MSC's New Training Initiative requires at least thirteen weeks off-the-job education and training. The money available for this is not sufficient to cover the cost of such a programme in further education colleges. Increasingly therefore the off-the-job education and training is going to competitive tenders from private schemes. Since the YTS schemes are in effect replacing traditional craft and operative courses, this would amount to a privatization of an important part of the public sector's contribution to education and training 16 to 19. Indeed this is having a dire effect on the public sector. Liverpool appointed staff at a cost of £750,000 to cope with YTS, for whom, however, no work could be found because fewer places were taken up in the public sector than were anticipated and more places were given to the cheaper employer-based training schemes. As John Pardoe, Director of a private training scheme, said with reference to retail and commercial training,

> B 2 (the college-based training programme) hasn't a chance in this field. The colleges just can't compete with us.

The government's sixty-nine skill centres, set up to provide occupational training for the adult unemployed, are to be turned into commercially run training businesses, competing with further education colleges for students.

Indirect subsidies through tax concessions

This is possibly the most significant way in which private schools receive public money. The charitable status of independent educational institutions releases them from paying *rates* that would otherwise be paid not only by other businesses but also by the local authority for its maintained schools, (charities, but not county schools, can claim a 50 per cent rate rebate); *taxes* on profits from fees charged (for example, the Girls' Public Day School Trust, a group of twenty-three schools, did in the year ending 31 August 1981 have a turnover of nearly £16m, made a profit of £1.3m and was exempted from any form of tax); and some *National Insurances*: charities, but not local authorities, can claim exemption from the employer's surcharge which is currently 3.5 per cent. Indeed, independent schools benefit from tax and rate relief to the tune of £22.5m — 3 per cent of their total income. At the same time charitable status enables fee payers to gain tax advantages through life insurance schemes, covenanting fees, annuities, etc. Furthermore independent schools run as charitable trusts hand out about £33m in scholarships and bursaries, about 5 per cent of the total fee income, nearly 7000 pupils benefiting. For example, Exeter School, in its

Appeal for the Eighties, Progress Report No. 1, puts the total sum raised so far at £150,000. Since a substantial amount of this comes from covenants or indeed from commerce and industry (for example, Barclays and National Westminster banks) and from various trust funds, then in effect the private sector is being heavily supported, quite unknowingly, by tax payers who have no opportunity to benefit from that private sector and indeed whose own children suffer from the effect it has upon the local maintained schools.

The charity laws benefit the private sector in other ways, too. Non-educational institutions — trust funds of various kinds — enable commercial and industrial bodies to support the private sector from money that otherwise would be taxed in the normal way. In Devon, for example, the St John Hospital Trust makes generous grants to independent and voluntary church schools. Such grants are particularly significant when they are put towards capital projects at a time when there is a much reduced capital programme for maintained schools.

There are many other ways in which taxpayers indirectly subsidize the private sector — fees for the children of employees that are put down to expenses (thus avoiding tax); the training of teachers for the private sector at public expense; the services of the inspectorate. The point is that in one way or another a large part of the private sector is being kept alive by public money — to such an extent that it can hardly be called an independent sector of education. The consequence of this is clear. Either the schools should free themselves from such dependence or they should accept the consequence of it, namely, the incorporation into the public sector, which increasingly is paying for its upkeep.

Hidden privatization from misuse of voluntary status

A third of our state schools are voluntary, almost all denominational. Most cooperate well with local county schools and their education authority. A small number, however — much criticized recently — try to run themselves as private schools on the rates. For example, voluntary comprehensive schools can misuse admissions prerogatives to select by attainment, social class, or race.

To solve such problems, including reduction of pupil numbers on an equal basis, harmonization of practice between county and voluntary schools is being urgently canvassed and steadily achieved.

This positive development could be much threatened, as could existing programmes of positive discrimination and multicultural education within the maintained sector, if schools for non-Christian minority religions or for ethnic minority groups were to be established separately by permitting existing private schools to be run on the rates as voluntary schools, or by taking over 'living' county schools and making them voluntary schools closed to all except one group.

Transfer of institutions and services into the private sector

The transfer of institutions and services to the private sector is now commonplace. The staff of Malvern Hills Adult Education College were dismissed and the College reestablished as a private charitable trust. Plans were being considered by the Ministry of Defence to put the employment of teachers in the armed forces into the hands of private agencies.

There is a statutory obligation upon LEAs to ensure the provision of school meals to those who want or need them. This obligation is normally satisfied through the authority's own catering service. Increasingly authorities are thinking of ways of handing over this, as well as other services, to private firms. In Merton, as in many other authorities, the school meals service has been handed over to a private firm. Similarly with cleaning which was privatized in Merton. The subsequent decline in services was so dramatic that the heads warned that children would have to stay at home because of the dirty conditions. What was lacking in the new arrangements was adequate staffing together with the commitment to a community of which the cleaners should be part.

Renting educational amenities

School buildings, which previously were available for extra-school and for community activities, are increasingly being restricted to activities that will at least cover their cost if not actually make a profit for the authority.

Selling educational amenities

A countryside survey by the Central Council of Physical Recreation showed that local authorities were planning to sell off 2370 acres of school playing fields, sports grounds, and leisure areas and this accords with Statutory Instrument 1981.909 of the Education (England and Wales) School Premises Regulation which amounted to a declaration that schools no longer needed as much playing field space as they once did. Sales of educational assets, including playing fields were forecast to be £55m in 1984.

Improverishing the Maintained Sector

Reduction of resources

Privatization is being promoted on the basis of extending the freedom of parents to choose. But genuine freedom requires viable, if different kinds of alternative. Freedom is a sham if one of the two alternatives is increasingly becoming unsatisfactory in educational terms through lack of resources. And this precisely is the judgment of Her Majesty's Inspectorate in its three annual reports on the effects of local authority expenditure on education. It points to unsatisfactory provision in many authorities on staffing, capitation, in-service, induction of new teachers, ancillary staff, advisory services, and maintenance of buildings — where 'satisfactory' means a level, range and balance of resources which HMI consider adequate for pupils to be taught 'according to their ages, abilities, and aptitudes'. Even if the cut-back in resources in the public sector at a time of increased financial support for the private sector is not part of the conscious policy of privatization, it has the same effect since many who can afford it are being driven to choose the private because of the inadequate resourcing of the public. A cheap way of implementing a policy of privatization!

Return to elementary school tradition

By 'elementary school tradition' I mean that the schools (i) are, by and large, run by a relatively privileged group of people for others', but not their own, children; and (ii) have a rather narrow curriculum that stresses the socially useful and the practical and denies access to wider cultural values and to the 'tools' of critical reflection. Privatization provides the conditions for the elementary tradition to flourish, whilst in turn being furthered by it. There is developing a significant curriculum break at 14 between those who pursue an essentially subject-based, academic course to GCE 'O' level and 'A' level and those who will be following 'pre-vocational' courses that stress the practical, the vocationally relevant, and the social and life skills. Increasingly we may see a curriculum break being encapsulated and an institutional break — the grammar type school in the subsidized private sector and the public sector concentrating upon the pre-vocational kind of course.

Non-support by management and political leaders

It is quite common for those responsible for running the public sector at every level — Secretary of State and leading politicians, chief education officers and area education officers, chairmen of education committees, school governors, even headteachers — to send their own offspring to the private sector. What is good enough for others' children is not good enough for their own. But the desertion by those responsible for managing the system affects the privatization of the system in three ways.

(i)   it indicates that what they are responsible for is not worth choosing;
(ii) it lowers the morale of teachers and parents who are trying to preserve the public sector as a viable alternative;
(iii) it removes from the public sector those who would otherwise be determined to make sure it is properly resourced.

Non-support from higher education

A disproportionate number of places in certain universities (Oxford, Cambridge, Exeter, for example) go to applicants from the private sector. This is likely to increase as the number of students chasing fewer places gets higher, because the cut-back in resources and staffing in the maintained sector denies to many children the opportunities for obtaining the very high grades demanded. Parents, wanting to provide the opportunity of a university education, may feel obliged to send their children to private schools.

Costing

The financial consequences of privatization are, as is made clear, only part of the concern. Nonetheless, they are important and need to be specified in some detail.

This, however, is not easy. The many indirect ways in which private education is subsidized although considerable, cannot be accurately measured on existing information. Indeed it is one purpose of this paper to start the process in which more precise information will be obtained. We do not know, for example, to what extent PTA and private funds are relied upon in different schools for essential resources. Nor do we know how many, and to what extent, charitable trusts support private education. It is difficult, too, to establish how much taxpayers' money is redirected to private sector through covenants, insurance policies, etc. Nonetheless, we do know that, together, the different developments do add up to a considerable investment of taxpayers' money in private education for the few and of the users' private money in essential public education for the many.

A conservative estimate of the minimum cost to the taxpayer of private education would be as follows:

	£m	
Assisted places	15	(increasing)
Government personnel (including travel subsidies)	70	(increasing)
Direct grant	10	(decreasing)
LEA purchase of places	30	(decreasing)
Youth training	25	(increasing)
Charity status (tax and rate loss)	50	
	£200m	

Conclusion

There is no doubting the direct payments and the increased subsidies given to the private sector of education. But this chapter aims to show that privatization is being achieved through many less direct and less obvious means — as part of a general social policy of shifting responsibility for essential services from government, at national and local levels, to the private individual, whilst at the same time giving financial support from public funds to that shift of responsibility.

It is important to note in this respect the gradual change in how private education is valued. Until recently it has been argued that individuals have the *right* to choose a private education for their children, should they so wish. But now what is at stake is the right, not simply to choose a private education, but to have it heavily subsidized by the taxpayer, even at the expense of the maintained sector.

The results of privatization in these many different shapes and forms are:

    (i)   a well balanced secondary education, suiting age, ability, and aptitude, available only to those who can pay for it (a) personally; or (b) as a group (for example, through fund-raising); or (c) through tax concessions open to a relatively few;

    (ii)   an impoverishment of the maintained sector of education and thus a reversal of the steady improvement we have witnessed since 1944;

    (iii)   the entrenchment of a two-tier system of curriculum — the more academic for the more privileged middle classes; the more practical and less well resourced for the rest, who are unable or unwilling to subscribe to the view that education is essentially a private matter.

The Sociology of the School: Streaming and Mixed Ability and Social Class

Stephen J. Ball

In the current political and economic context, the struggle in schools to achieve more democratic forms of comprehensive education seems, with a few notable exceptions[1], to have been brought to an end. Indeed, with the public agenda for discussion of educational issues tightly defined by the populist policies of the Conservative government and schools being subject to the pressures and constraints of 'market forces', regression rather than progress would seem to typify the climate in many secondary schools. Furthermore, this gloomy scenario must also take account of the difficulties being created by the impact of falling rolls and the undoubted state of low morale which is general throughout the teaching workforce. Schools and teachers are on the defensive, and locally they are in competition with one another for parents and pupils. According to Lightfoot (1978) as the pressure of this competition continues

> ... a downward spiral can be anticipated ... one of lowering morale, distrust, institutional friction and that debilitation which comes from the feeling that futures can scarcely be influenced and cannot be controlled. (p. 38)

It is not surprising, therefore, that issues relating to the democratic development of the comprehensive school that were being addressed seriously in the 1960s and early 70s have now been eclipsed by the more immediate problems of institutional survival. The battering received by schools and teachers since the 'Great Debate' onwards has, in some cases, produced a state of anoesis.

But while these issues may have been wiped off the political agenda in many schools, at least for the time being, educational pressure groups and educational researchers cannot allow them to be totally neglected in continuing debate. One such set of issues, cast to the sidelines in the present defensive climate, concerns the grouping of pupils in schools and specifically the debate over the merits of streaming versus mixed-ability grouping. In any consideration of the role of social class in secondary education this must be a matter of prime consideration. Research done during the 1960s and 1970s demonstrated repeatedly the strong and enduring relationships between streaming and social class differentiation. Douglas' (1964) studies of the careers of primary age children in streamed schools found that when children of the same level of measured ability were considered

> middle class children tend to be allocated to the upper streams and the manual working-class children to the lower ones (there are 11 per cent more middle-class children in the upper streams than would be expected from their measured ability at eight years and 26 per cent fewer in the lower). (p. 148)

Hargreaves (1967) found a similar relationship in his secondary modern school, as also did Lacey (1970) in his grammar school study. In my own analysis (1981) of a banded comprehensive school, *Beachside*, I found a considerable over-representation of middle class children in band one and a concomitant under-representation in band two.

Streaming

These findings have implications both in terms of the immediate school experiences of different groups of pupils moving through the education system and for the longer-term personal and social futures of these different groups and for society more generally. I will attempt to sketch out some of these implications in four areas: (i) the allocation and distribution of initial life chances to pupils; (ii) the impact of streaming on the social relations between pupils; (iii) the creation of separate institutional sub-worlds in which pupils experience their education; and (iv) consequences for the social atmosphere and sense of community of the school.

The Allocation and Distribution of Initial Life Chances to Pupils

While discussions about the decision to stream or not to stream are most often conducted around the problems that may be faced by some teachers who feel that their subject does not lend itself to mixed-ability teaching, the profound effects of streaming on the initial life chances of pupils are usually ignored. It should be recognized that the separation of pupils into streams or bands or sets has as powerful a predictive effect on their school careers and post school opportunities as did the earlier separation into grammar and secondary modern schools.

The allocation to streams also entails an allocation to particular institutional identities. Given the assumption of homogenity which accompanies thinking about streaming it is perhaps not surprising that individual pupils find themselves typified with the labels used to identify their stream. Each stream label carries its own particular status within the school and staff frequently work with strongly institutional-ized and therefore preconceived notions about the typical 'A' stream or band three child. Such labels are embedded aspects of the shared meanings that teacher rely on in their everyday work with pupils. For individual pupils these labels represent powerful limitations upon the sorts of social and academic identity that they can achieve or aspire to in school and yet they derive from fairly arbitrary lines of demarcation between pupils. As Keddie (1971) suggests, 'what a teacher knows about pupils derives from the organizational device of banding or streaming' (p. 139).

Some indication of the phenomenological power of grouping structures, particularly in relation to teachers' perceptions of pupils, can be gleaned from a comparison of the streaming system at Lumley Secondary Modern (Hargreaves, 1967), Hightown Grammar (Lacey, 1970) and Beachside Comprehensive (Ball, 1981). Hightown Grammar was a four-form entry school admitting approximately 15 per cent of the 11 year-olds in Hightown from each cohort. The pupils were streamed from the beginning of the second year (2E an express stream taking 'O' levels a year early plus 2A, B and C). By the end of the second year the 'climates' in the different classes were quite distinct; 2C were regarded by their peers and their teachers as bullies and 'tough eggs', 'they are aggressive, loud-mouthed and feared by many who are successful in terms of the dominant school norms' (p. 65). One of the teachers explained bluntly to Lacey about 2C, 'There's not one boy in the class who has any sort of academic ability. In fact, most of them shouldn't be in the school at all. It's not fair on them and it's not fair on the school' (p. 67). The blanket use of stream typing is very clear in this statement, as this teacher sees it the boys of 2C are of a kind, they are written off as a whole, he does not see them as a group of diverse individuals but as an undifferentiated 2C type. Lumley secondary

modern was responsible for pupils who had failed on their 11+ scores
to get a grammar school place. Here the boys were placed in one of five
streams (A to E) from the beginning of the first year. At the beginning
of the fourth year 4A consisted of those pupils who would be taking
CSE examinations. 4A was dominated by an expressed concern with
academic achievement, a high standard of physical hygiene and dress
was maintained and high attendance was the norm. The pupils
themselves and their teachers regarded 4A as providing the academic
leadership in the school. Teachers also regarded 4A as rewarding to
teach. The low stream boys despised 4A 'for being academically
oriented, hardworking, teachers' favourites, posh and cowardly'
(p. 71). Beachside Comprehensive was a mixed school, taking all the
pupils from the Beachside community (with the exception of those
attending private schools, about 2 per cent of any cohort). Beachside
the first year. In each cohort approximately 45 per cent of the intake
were assigned to band 1 classes. The teachers' perceptions and expectations of the normal band 1 pupil is captured in the following
composite.

The band 1 child

> has academic potential . . . will do 'O' levels . . . and a good
> number will stay on to the sixth-form . . . likes doing projects
> . . . knows what the teacher wants . . . is bright, alert and
> enthusiastic . . . can concentrate . . . produces neat work . . . is
> interested . . . wants to get on . . . is grammar school material
> . . . you can have discussions with . . . friendly . . . has common
> sense.

These images and impressions were matched by the pupils' own
sense of commitment to academic values and school norms. The moral
climate of the band 1 classroom supported hard work and positive
attitudes towards school and teachers. One girl who had been promoted out of band 2 into band 1, described her new class as

> much nicer, they are much more friendly; it was horrible in the
> other form. They weren't nice people. I had friends but I used
> to get higher marks and they called me a 'creep' and things.
> They seemed much older in this form when I came in.

All the band 1 pupils at Beachside were the 'best' pupils in the
school, and they reflected 'best pupil' attitudes and behaviour back at
the teachers.[2] The significant point is that in terms of comparison with
Hightown and Lumley all of the grammar school pupils and some at

least of 4A would be included in this group. And yet the attitudes and aspirations of the band 1 pupils parallel most directly those evident in the grammar school express stream. The identity of these pupils is to a great extent an artifact of the grouping system employed. The status system of bands, the pupils' self image and the teachers' attitudes and behaviour towards them combine in a powerful process of definition and reaction. The very opposite effect is achieved by the same process at work in reverse with the lower bands, as we shall see.

The effects of these stream-based identities are perhaps most crucial in the role they play in the channelling decisions which come later in the pupils' school careers. Their use in the organization and processing of pupils is perhaps most clear cut in the allocation of pupils to option groups at 14+. At this point the streaming of pupils in the first three years of secondary school (or some part of those first three years) is decisively related to the certification of them for entry into the job market, such as it is, or further education. Access to high status knowledge areas (academic subjects at 'O' level) which have high negotiable value outside the school is denied to those pupils who by virtue of their allocation to low stream groups have 'inappropriate' profiles and identities. The idea of 'appropriate' choices is very much an extrapolation of the streamed identities that pupils acquire in their earlier school career. It is important to note that access to 'O' level courses may be also guarded by teachers who have one eye on the maintenance of 'acceptable' pass-rates at the end of the course.

Woods (1979) summarizes the option choice process and its implicit relationship to social class differentiation in the following way.

> With these powerful forces structuring their policies and activities, teachers 'mediate' the choosing arena, making the rules and provide most of the equipment (including the pupil's own view of himself) for the game of subject choice. For them the game is to guide pupils into the right channels to get the bell of examination results to ring. The criteria that they use are past achievement and future potential. For all these factors we know that there is a strong connection with social class, though it is not a simple one. The middle classes are at home in this arena, the working classes strangers. (p. 61)

Despite the notions of equality of opportunity that have been attached to the reorganization of comprehensive education, the internal organization of those schools which operate with streaming maintains a system of selection which in its implications for pupils' life chances is as decisive as the grammar/secondary modern division. Halsey (1974) makes the point that 'What one is taught may be of importance to one's future position in society, but what one is taught depends very largely on who one is, i.e. one's social class antecedents'.

In this way systems of streaming in the comprehensive school contribute to the process of the reproduction of class relations through education. The streams channel and differentiate pupils and provide them with different educational experiences, delivering them eventually at a point of entry into the labour market or into unemployment with differentiated skills, competences, publically certified identities and sense of their own worth and capabilities. Education does not entirely determine their future life chances but certainly exercises considerable constraint upon the range of initial possibilities that confront them.

The Impact of Streaming on the Social Relations between Pupils

According to Anthony Crosland one of the primary reasons for establishing a system of comprehensive education in Britain would be to ameliorate some of the social divisions and conflicts that are embodied in and reproduced by the bipartite system. But significantly Crosland (1956) saw no logical relationship between comprehensive education and mixed-ability grouping. He believed that simply by bringing all pupils from all social classes (always leaving aside the continued existence of the public schools) into one school that greater tolerance and mutual understanding would follow.

> The object of having comprehensive schools is not to abolish all competition and all envy, which might be rather a hopeless task, but to avoid the extreme social division caused by physical segregation into schools of widely divergent status, and the extreme social resentment caused by failure to win a grammar (or, in future, public) school place, when this is thought to be the only avenue to a 'middle-class' occupation. That division and that resentment bear no relation whatever to the effects of grading *within* a single school, with the possibility of regrading at any time simply by moving across a corridor. (p. 272)

He could not have been more wrong. It is clear that the effect of streaming is to produce a *polarized* social structure among pupils. That is to say they tend to choose friends from within their own stream or from adjacent streams and to develop hostile and antipathetic attitudes towards those pupils who inhabit the opposite extreme of the streaming system. This is most simply illustrated from the friendship choices made by pupils in the streamed secondary modern school investigated by Hargreaves (1967, p. 7) (see figure 1).

Figure 1

		RECIPIENT							
	Form	*4A*	*4B*	*4C*	*4D*	*4E*	*Others*	*N*	*Mean choices per boy*
DONOR	4A	78	12	2	0	2	7	113	3.8
	4B	11	77	6	1	0	5	99	3.5
	4C	2	7	70	17	1	2	83	3.6
	4D	1	1	23	60	8	7	75	3.4

Figures are percentages.

The process underlying this separation is one of sub-cultural formation. The development of pro-school attitudes and commitments among top stream groups and the rejection of and alientation from such attitudes and commitments among the anti-school, low stream groups. The pupils who find themselves allocated to low stream, low status positions, and regarded as failures within the formal normative culture of the school, will have a vested interest in distancing themselves from this formal culture. They will seek status recovery elsewhere, through the celebration of toughness, classroom disruption and work avoidance or by importing pop-media, football, ethnic, or working-class shop-floor cultures from arenas of experience outside of school.

These low stream, anti-school groups come to see their top-stream counterparts as 'poofs', 'weeds' and 'wets' who are boring, have no fun and 'suck up to teachers'. The top stream look down on the anti-school pupils as 'dummies', 'thickos' and 'only interested in pop-music and football'. As Willis (1977) has pointed out so cogently, this sort of separation has other effects, the rejection of the formal school culture by anti-school pupils is also a rejection of mental, in favour of manual, labour and is part of the process, in which the pupils themselves are thereby implicated, by which working class pupils get working class jobs. Here then the comprehensive school is not contributing in a positive way to greater tolerance in society as a whole, but rather it is feeding and perpetuating social divisions and social conflicts. It is obviously difficult to measure or isolate the damage that is being done by schools in this way but clearly these divisions and antipathies provide no sort of basis for social solidarity beyond school. We have to add to this picture the fact that the formal culture of the school celebrates (often literally) and rewards individual mobility and rivalry through competition. This also has its effects on the social relations between pupils in the same streams and classes. Pupils learn neither the skills nor the virtues or possibilities of corporate effect, except in the very negative senses outlined above.

The Creation of Separate Institutional Sub-worlds in which Pupils Experience their Education

The separation of pupils into streams does not involve only a differentiation by status and a process of institutional channelling, it also gives rise to a whole series of other qualitative differences in the pupils' experience of school. These include curricular and syllabus differences, and pedagogic and relational differences. Curricular differences are normally institutionalized to provide course work and materials 'best suited' to the different educational 'capabilities' of the pupils. For example, this may involve following different courses in mathematics and French using different textbooks. The level of conceptual difficulty and/or the pace of coverage of syllabus topics differ for pupils in different streams. Clearly, it is difficult to argue that all pupils could and should cover the same material at the same pace throughout their school careers. There is a wide range of differences between individuals in 'their ability to listen, concentrate and understand; ... as to critical thinking, their sensitivity to criticism, their acuity of perception and their tolerance of the tedious; they will differ as to their interests, their pleasures, their capacity to discriminate and to reason' (Bailey and Bridges, 1983, p. 49). The problem with streaming is that it institutionalizes this variety of differences across subjects and through time. Movements between streams are minimal and as Douglas (1964) found, 'once allocated, the children tend to take on the characteristics expected of them and the forecasts of ability made at the point of streaming are to this extent self-fulfilling' (p. 147). This self-fulfilment operates in a number of ways. It is evident for example in the reaction formation process occurring among the pupils, as described above. As the low stream pupils react against the school and the teachers they tend to confirm the academic judgments upon which streaming is based. If they avoid class work, refuse homework, lose or deface their books, 'forget' equipment, come late and are more often absent than other pupils, they are unlikely to achieve the sort of academic performance that would cause teachers to revize their assumptions about the relationship between stream and ability. Self-fulfilment is also built into the formal and informal syllabus differences between streams. Having spent time following different course materials at a different pace of work it becomes more and more difficult to allow movement between streams. As far as the allocation to options is concerned, as discussed previously, low stream pupils may find themselves disbarred from consideration for some courses at 'O' level or CSE because they have not covered topics in the first three years that teachers define as necessary qualifications for entry. At Beachside (Ball, 1981) these sorts of syllabus differences were also related to significant pedagogic differences between band 1 and band 2 classes. For the teacher of the band 1 form, classroom problems were primarily related to the teaching process; the organization and preparation of material, the coverage of the syllabus and preparation of pupils for tests and examinations. The great majority of teacher 'talk' and interaction with the pupils was concerned with subject material or the clarification of work tasks. In the case of the band 2 lessons, the teacher's major concerns were often not those of instruction but those of control. Discussion was far less commonly used in band 2 lessons, and there was a lot more copying from the board and exercise work. The teachers spent much longer talking in band 1 lessons and mentioned that they less often felt the need to reiterate basic principles. As one human studies teacher put it 'Band 2 lessons are essentially dull for both teachers and pupils'.

Again closely bound up with these pedagogical differences were important relational differences. First, as I have indicated, the band 2 lessons were frequently dominated by regulation rather than instruction and the teachers found it necessary to modify their teacher-methods accordingly. Second, implicit in the stereotypes of band identity which the teachers operated with was not only a sense of difference between the bands but also a moral evaluation. Generally, the teachers considered band 1 pupils to be more like themselves and more satisfying and worthwhile to teach. Over several years of secondary schooling the relationships between band 2 pupils and their teachers tended to be strained and often hostile. Teachers were most concerned with what they perceived as the negative characteristics of band 2 pupils. Their perceptions were linked with expectations that they had of appropriate classroom behaviour. Expectations to which the band 2 pupils failed to conform. Again it is difficult to measure in any meaningful way what the impact of these sorts of relationships, extended over a period of several years, might be, either on pupils or teachers. But it would seem unlikely to form very positive attitudes towards school and education for the band 2 pupils to pass onto their own children. In all these senses both pupils and teachers are 'victims' of the streaming system. Once streaming is 'done' both have to live with the consequences.

The Social Atmosphere and Sense of Community in the School

It should already be very clear that streaming in various ways has a deleterious impact on the social atmosphere and sense of community in a school. It is a source of conflict between pupils and between pupil and teachers. It gives rise to the alienation of groups of pupils from the institution of school and from the learning process. As I have suggested low stream pupils will see themselves as having a vested interest in devaluing the goals and defacing the fabric of the institution which accredits them as failures. This is graphically clear in the incidence of graffiti and vandalism evident in many schools. Indeed it is difficult to imagine how any organization could expect to maintain the loyalty and commitment of groups of people it is in the process of labelling as inadequate.

It is not difficult to understand why it is that these aspects of streaming seem to have provided the strongest basis of interest and support among teachers for mixed-ability grouping. The ILEA (1976) and DES (1978) surveys of mixed-ability teaching both found that pragmatic reasoning about the possibilities of improved classroom relations and social atmosphere provided the strongest basis of support for the abolition of streaming. This was also the case in the survey of seventeen Greater London education authorities reported by Davies (1977). It was found that:

> The great common denominator is a desire to get away from the worst features of streaming. These are most sharply focused upon as the production of demoralized, demotivated, unteach-able middle school groups, bad for themselves, their teachers and other children. A suburban near-balanced intake boys' school head put it succinctly: first and partial second-year mixed

ability was adopted so as to 'avoid a rejected group because it would affect the work of the whole school and not just those kids'. He, no doubt, in common with the head of a comprehensive school with a rather more beleaguered and cosmopolitan past, wanted to avoid continuing a situation where 'band two curricula became a defeated area in terms of resources and staff interest which meant frustration for kids quite apart from the social stigma'. These sorts of sentiments tend to owe a great deal more to hard-won experience and a sensibility as to the real constraints and possibilities which hedge about schools, than to ideological fervour. (p. 27)

Mixed-Ability

If motives of this kind are to the fore when schools do abandon streaming in favour of mixed-ability grouping it can be expected that many of the assumptions and practices of the streamed classroom will be carried over into the new teaching situation. Furthermore, for many of those involved in such changes destreaming is primarily seen as organizational matter, the introduction of mixed-ability *grouping*, rather than a pedagogic matter, the introduction of mixed-ability *teaching*. Obviously, the extent to which teaching methods are changed to respond to the new classroom situation varies from school to school and subject to subject. But on the whole some subject teachers have been more willing to rethink their working methods than others. With English and humanities teachers more likely to see the need for radical shifts in curriculum and pedagogy and mathematics and language teachers less likely to see such a need. In particular schools these subject-based differences can give rise to a considerable diversity of ways of working in the classroom and provide the basis for enduring conflict over the costs and benefits of mixed-ability. In Barker-Lunn's (1970) terms we might divide teachers crudely into 'streamers' and 'non-streamers' and consider her findings concerning the work of 'streamers' in unstreamed schools.

Only about half the staff in non-streamed schools could be called 'non-streamers'. The others held attitudes more typical of teachers in streamed schools. This finding is important, for this group of teachers appeared to create a 'streamed atmosphere' within their non-streamed classes. Their teaching methods, their lessons and their attitudes tended to reflect the pattern found in streamed schools. They even streamed their children so that different ability groups were seated in different parts of the classroom. They seemed to be counteracting consciously or unconsciously, the aims of the non-streamed schools. (pp. 272–3)

These findings were reflected in the analysis of the introduction of mixed-ability grouping at Beachside Comprehensive. What emerged from an initial examination of the responses of the various subject departments to the teaching of mixed-ability groups was a continuum of positions stretching between the polarized views of the English and languages departments. With the English Department represented by a cluster of attitudes and commitments approximating to what Barker-Lunn calls 'child-centred', 'with a greater concern for the all-round development of each pupil' (p. 273) and the Languages Department represented by a cluster of attitudes and commitments that approximate to what Barker-Lunn calls 'knowledge-centred'; 'for these teachers the emphasis was on the acquisition of knowledge and the attainment of set academic standards they were particularly interested in and concerned for the bright child' (p. 273). The attitudes to mixed-ability and willingness to change methods of the different subject groups are represented in Figure 2.

For a variety of reasons then we cannot take the abandonment of streaming as an indication of radical changes in teachers' thinking about their pupils or as necessarily associated with the re-working of teaching methods. But the continuance of streamed thinking and teaching is not simply a matter of the rigidity of teachers. Bearing down on the grouping arrangements of any secondary school, streamed or mixed-ability, are the constraints and demands of the examination system. A system which was designed for and which perpetuates a bipartite education. The demands of the 'O' level syllabuses in particular percolate down into the first three years of the secondary school and in certain subjects dictate areas of content and pace of coverage. Such demands are in basic conflict with the immediate problems of teaching mixed-ability classes.

It is not simply that difficulties arise in attempting to sponsor and prepare some pupils within the mixed-ability classroom for 'O' level courses they might take later in their school career, but typically the introduction of mixed-ability is accompanied by close scrutiny of the 'academic implications' of the change. Some parents view mixed-

Figure 2.

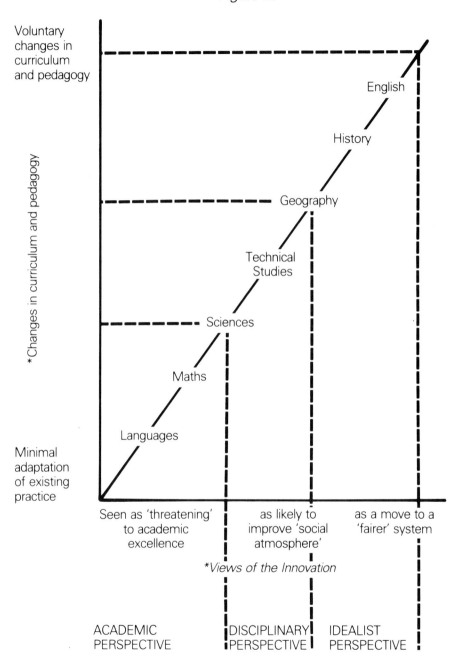

These are not quantitative variables.

ability grouping as a threat to the chances that their child may have of passing examinations at 16+. Individual subject departments may be jealously safeguarding 'O' level pass-rates achieved on the basis of streaming and early selection. Headteachers are likely to be sensitive to the way in which a move to mixed-ability grouping affects the public image and reputation of their school. All of these factors draw particular attention to the 'needs of the brighter child', and can put pressure on the classroom teacher who is seeking ways of working with mixed-ability groups. In other words, the resolution of pedagogic dilemmas in the mixed-ability classroom is by no means achieved in a vacuum. The teacher is hedged in by 'frames' and constraints which limit the range of possibilities for action and pressures and demands which dictate or preempt a whole variety of planning decisions. It should perhaps then not come as a surprise to discover that many teachers resolve these classroom dilemmas by continuing to rely on whole-class teaching methods or close equivalents (see Ball, 1980). As the HMI report (1978) recorded 'While we found ... mixed-ability grouping we had greater difficulty in finding mixed-ability teaching'. Sands (1982) explains this very simply, she argues that 'For many teachers most of the time, a class lesson is easier, neater and less demanding' (p. 58). She provides an interesting comparison of the working-methods of eight teachers considered by their headteachers or other observers as 'effective' teachers of mixed-ability groups. They were observed on a number of occasions teaching first year secondary mixed-ability classes and figure 3 shows the proportion of time each devoted to group work, individualized learning and whole class teaching. (Unfortunately we are not told which subjects they teach.)

Bearing in mind the existence of these pressures and constraints the question to be asked now is, what are the implications of mixed-ability grouping for pupils from different social class backgrounds? As with most questions of this kind there is no clear cut or short answer, rather, drawing on the findings of the Beachside study, a number of contradictory tendencies are evident. First, by definition the pupils are no longer physically separated or selected early for different formal careers through the school. However, data on friendship choice does indicate that pupils from the same social class background are more likely to choose each other as friends and this is increasingly likely as they move through the school. Second, while the creation of mixed-ability groups breaks down the pre-existing typifications of pupils based on structural identities, requiring teachers to 'make' rather than 'take' their own evaluations of individual pupils, teachers did approach their mixed-

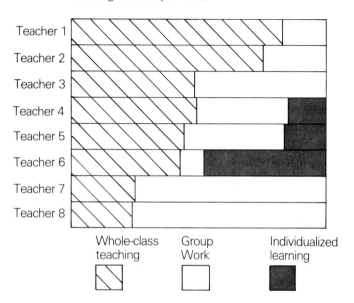

Figure 3. Eight teachers and mixed-ability classes: teaching modes (per cent)

ability classes with strong expectations of finding a three-fold categorization of ability, bright-average-weak, normally distributed in each group. Third, the concerns about 'the progress of the brighter child' and the effect of mixed-ability on academic standards, created a situation of heightened awareness about relative levels of achievement. The teachers became very concerned about identifying the 'ability' of individual pupils as quickly as possible. In some senses it might even be said that the criteria which were used to evaluate or categorize pupils were narrowed rather than broadened by the introduction of mixed-ability. Fourth, in those subjects where the teaching methods and curriculum were not adapted in any significant way to the mixed-ability situation, for example in French, the differences between pupils became apparent very quickly. By treating the pupils as though they were alike these teachers heightened the differences between them by employing methods and working at a pace suitable to only some. As Bailey and Bridges (1983) argue 'it is *not* just to treat pupils as though they were exactly alike. Indeed to do so would be unjust' (p. 29). Fifth, perversely, it can also be argued that those subjects that were individualizing and differentiating curricula and learning within the classroom were also acting unjustly, especially where such individualization was linked to the preparation for different courses at 14+, in mathematics for example. Again, Bailey and Bridges note that 'There is *prima facie* conflict ... between the concern for individuality and the concern for equality' (p. 24). But as I have noted previously, the first priority expressed by teachers who support mixed-ability is most commonly a concern to improve discipline and social atmosphere, not to promote greater equality. Although I would presume that few would be opposed to this as a useful and healthy outcome of mixed-ability. Pedagogical adaptations to mixed-ability grouping are first and foremost pragmatic responses to and methods of coping with a new and problematic teaching situation. Teachers are concerned in the first instance to achieve an effective and workable balance between the most immediate classroom goals of order and instruction. Individualized, or individuated[3], methods, like the use of work sheets, are probably the most straightforward means of achieving this balance in the mixed-ability classroom. Sixth, alongside the processes of evaluation and individuation there is also a process of differentiation at work. Through the award of marks, the reinforcement of 'goodwork', and the distribution of informal cues, pupils are made aware of their relative status and worth. They are in competition with one another for the limited success roles available in the classroom — getting top marks for homework, coming in the top six in the end-of-term exam, getting all answers right in a test, being form captain, etc. Such competition rarely takes account of the unequal resources available to the pupils.

It is in these ways that differences between pupils in terms of social class culture, linguistic ability, motivation parental support and encouragement become relevant in terms of differential performance and these are translated into a differential allocation of rewards and status. Thus, again somewhat perversely, the introduction of mixed-ability at Beachside, robbed some working-class pupils of the opportunity to experience those minor success roles that would have been available to them in the band 2 classroom where they would not have been in direct competition with well-resourced and supported middle class pupils. The relationship between social class and examination achievement was very strong in the two mixed-ability case-study classes I investigated in detail at Beachside (see table 1).

Finally, in the individuated mixed-ability classroom, the teacher becomes a scarce resource. Pupils must compete for the teacher's time and attention. Not all pupils may be equally well equipped for this competition and some may find the skills involved in working independently without direction for long periods of time hard to come by. Certainly Martin (1971) asserts that

Table 1

Exam. positions	Middle-class	Working class
1–10	10	–
11–20	3	7
21–9	1	8
Total	14	15

Table 8.10: Covariation of exam position and social class: 1LN

Exam. positions	Middle-class	Working-class	Unclassified
1–10	7	3	–
11–20	3	6	1
21–8	1	7	–
Totals	11	16	1

Methods of teaching which aim at letting each child move at his own pace give middle-class children an even greater advantage over their working-class contemporaries since the involvement of parents in teaching basic skills and providing intellectual stimulation can be a crucial determinant of a child's 'natural pace'. (p. 295)

While the first phase of secondary schooling remains a preparation for the next phase, the examination courses begun at 14+, it is highly likely that the system of grouping pupils will be constrained and contaminated by problems of curriculum coverage and pace which put some pupils at a distinct disadvantage. The defining characteristics of this first phase remain essentially as *selection* and *competition*, some are selected and others rejected and in any competition there are failures. In our school system rejection and failure continue to be strongly associated with social class.

Notes

1 The recent initiatives in the ILEA in relation to the underperformance of girls, ethnic minorities and working-class pupils would be one example of continuing attempts to move towards more democratic forms of schooling.

2 There were a handful of exceptions, those pupils who found themselves as failures in the band 1 context. But they had very little impact on the overall

pattern or climate of band 1 lessons (see *Beachside Comprehensive*, pp. 81–90).

3 Individualization occurs when specific tasks, materials and programmes are produced for individual pupils according to their learning needs and problems. Individuation occurs when the pupils are presented with the same tasks, materials and programmes but work individually and perhaps at their own pace.

References

BAILEY, C. and BRIDGES, D. (1983) *Mixed-Ability Grouping*, London, George Allen and Unwin.

BALL, S.J. (1980) 'Mixed-ability teaching: The worksheet method', *British Journal of Educational Technology*, 11, 1.

BALL, S.J. (1981) *Beachside Comprehensive*, Cambridge, Cambridge University Press.

BARKER-LUNN, J. (1970) *Streaming in Primary Schools*, Windsor, NFER.

CROSLAND, A. (1956) *The Future of Socialism*, London, Cape.

DAVIES, B. (1977) 'Meanings and motives in "going mixed-ability"' in DAVIES, B. and CAVE, R.G. (Eds) *Mixed Ability Teaching in the Secondary School*, London, Ward Lock.

DEPARTMENT OF EDUCATION AND SCIENCE (1978) *Matters for Discussion No. 6 Mixed-ability Work in Comprehensive Schools*, London, HMSO.

DOUGLAS, J.W.B. (1964) *The Home and the School*, London, MacGibbon and Kee.

HALSEY, A.H. (1974) 'Education and social mobility in Britain since World-War II' O.E.C.D. paper, Paris.

HARGREAVES, D.H. (1967) *Social Relations in a Secondary School*, London, Routledge and Kegan Paul.

ILEA (1976) *Mixed-Ability Grouping: Report of an ILEA Inspectorate Survey*, London, ILEA.

LACEY, C. (1970) *Hightown Grammar: The School as a Social System*, Manchester, Manchester University Press.

LIGHTFOOT, M. (1978) 'The educational consequences of falling rolls', in RICHARDS, C. (Ed.) *Power and the Curriculum*, Driffield, Nafferton.

MARTIN, B. (1971) 'Progressive education versus the working classes', *Critical Quarterly*, 13, pp. 297–320.

SANDS, M. (1982) 'Teaching methods: myth and reality' in KERRY, T. and SANDS, M. (Eds) *Mixed-Ability Teaching*, London, Croom Helm.

WILLIS, P. (1977) *Learning to Labour*, Farnborough, Saxon House.

WOODS, P.E. (1979) *The Divided School*, London, Routledge and Kegan Paul.

Education and Social Class: Privatization and the Sociology of the School: Discussion

The issues of privatization and the sociology of the school are aptly paired. Privatization focuses on the totality of the education system and Richard Pring argues against the diversion of resources to a privileged top stream of schools segregated by fee-paying, which reflects and perpetuates social class divisions. Stephen Ball looks at one of the smallest units within the system — the individual classroom — and argues against grouping pupils by streaming where class divisions are reinforced and pupils outside the top streams harmed by the lower expectations we have of them and they have of themselves.

Peter Mortimore's chapter adds a powerful, overall indictment of the system which calls for changes in education. There is great variety within social classes as well as between them. The dramatic differences in class composition between the Open University entry and entry to other forms of higher education could well be because social class designation is differently made. Were it to be assessed on the same basis, it is likely to be more like the polytechnic entry. The use of catch-up mechanisms like the OU may also be suspect because they become dominated by the middle class. This, however, should not invalidate the practice of providing such routes through education, and many more are needed.

In addition, since the 1970s a new grouping of unemployed has appeared whose educational chances have to be assessed. These are poor and the group is disproportionately working class. There are also the petty rulings which prevent the young unemployed returning to school or college after 16 without losing supplementary benefit. Such a system once again penalizes what is almost entirely a working-class group for seeking education.

Although all classes were being 'jacked up' before 1979, since that time they are all being 'jacked down'. A.H. Halsey's theory of 'two stage reform' maintains that in stage one the middle class rush in to occupy the spaces created, but in stage two there is saturation and the working class begins to increase its presence, along with women and minority groups. This was about to happen on a large scale by 1979, but along came the economic slump and the cutbacks, and the movement was killed. It was a breakthrough which never materialized.

Both Pring and Ball present powerful arguments for opposing streaming in all its forms — whether it be setting or the existence of a separate, private education sector. It is regrettable that the investigation into streaming and mixed ability has virtually ceased and the issue little discussed. Research shows that the top attainers are not harmed by destreaming while middle and low attainers often show significant improvement. The gap does narrow.

Nonetheless, destreaming does continue especially at the point of entry to comprehensive education; although more setting does take place later on to prepare for exams.

Mixed ability has its own pitfalls, one of which is streaming within a mixed-ability class: the 'top table' practice of so many primary schools. It also has to be recognized that mixed ability teaching is difficult and teachers must be helped to do it well. Resources are needed to help schools to destream. Certainly where poor mixed ability teaching does occur, it discredits the whole practice. It is a skill which requires a lot of learning. There is also some disagreement about whether teaching groups can be genuinely random or whether they need a few pace-setting high attainers present in each teaching group.

Mixed ability is often adopted because it lowers the level of social conflict in a school rather than because teachers feel it will promote learning. It is still not clear whether this really does influence post-school solidarity between social groups or merely masks conflict during the school years. Stephen Ball cites the objective of destreaming as the promotion of social solidarity beyond the school and of a corporate identity across all social classes. Others feel that cooperative activity might be a better objective. However, real group work towards developing a corporate identity in experiential learning can be a valuable means of encouraging personal development.

Richard Pring believes that the private sector can co-exist with the state and all that is at present wrong is that resources due to state schools are being diverted to the private sector. Once restored to the state and once proper support for state education comes, Pring claims, the private sector will present no threat. This seems doubtful.

The reasons for parents wanting private education tend to be power, social exclusiveness and personal development. The first two are unacceptable but the last is a positive desire any education system should promote.

One significant area of disagreement is often whether to develop a provision for alternative schooling in a reformed or ideal comprehensive system. Some take the view that we must listen to the 'messages' coming from those dissatisfied with mainstream education or who want schools for their own cultures or minority religions. Such schools would not, it is claimed, be in opposition to comprehensive education, but rather alternative to it.

Advocates of alternatives also claim that if community schooling becomes the norm, private education is impossible since no fee-paying school can be a community school.

Others claim this would be a dangerous development, lead to yet more segregation, damage the majority's schooling, and merely create a new way for the middle class to reassert its monopoly over education within any reformed system.

However, if individual comprehensives want to develop in alternative ways — and their parents, teachers and local communities agree — this is perhaps a possible way forward. Certainly a variety of models for comprehensive education are needed. Experiments in private schools are largely 'wild-cat' and no pointer to good practice. In state, locally supported schools such experiments could be a useful indicator for new directions. They could be closely monitored and 'controlled' by setting out a series of guidelines.

Only a genuine community school, where those involved in a school agree together to move in a particular direction, might solve this dilemma.

Just as changes in school organization, such as destreaming can make a difference and start development in a new direction, so too would ending the larger divisions of private versus public education in the organization of the system as a whole. Ending private education though is a negative idea. It is better to put the change in terms of moving from a stratified national system of schools to a new network of education where all schools serve their own communities, and in a much wider way than in the past.

For there to be any chance of narrowing the social class gap and enhancing school success, there must — along with destreaming — be a reform of the curriculum and examinations, moving away from subject-centred learning, short time modules, and exam-dominated courses towards other ways of organizing time, knowledge and assessment.

One recurring theme in discussions on reform is that one change alone is unlikely to be enough. Each strategy for change has merit, but it is the combination of changes — each supporting and being promoted by the other — that is necessary. Only a multiple strategy will do to counter the effects of multiple deprivation.

Both profiles and graded tests are worth considering, albeit with caution since the middle class can dominate these in the same way as previous forms of assessment. Such criteria could just become new forms of labelling, leaving the system basically unchanged.

Other strategies for change include ending the practice of a curriculum made up of narrow building blocks of discrete subjects and moving to wider approaches of learning. There is the Scandinavian practice where knowledge is organized into a few broad areas (natural, social, personal) and pupils negotiate programmes of study with teachers after 16. Up to 14 there is no assessment of any kind. From 14 to 16 there is a common curriculum for all with only a limited in-school set of tests with one aggregate mark.

Though not all of this should necessarily be endorsed, 'knowledge as parcels' is a limited approach that stratifies schooling and minimizes success, dividing pupils along class lines (through 'option choice') as surely as does streaming.

Some defensive action is needed too. For example, most initiatives under the TVEI scheme threaten the principle of comprehensive education through the 'vocationalization' of a large group from the age of 14 while the academic pupils are left to get on with their full comprehensive schooling and move up the traditional ladder of success. Only by local community effort, involving the non-vocational groups in the whole work of the school, refusing to permit the vocational to be hived off, can schools protect themselves from this threat.

A further threat is to accept that until change comes nothing can be done. Exams, as presently organized, have to be accepted, but much can be done to mitigate their damaging effect on the majority's education — for example, choosing exams for CSE and GCE which are so close in syllabus content that classes can be taught together after 14 rather than separately.

All such strategies have to be supported widely in society. None is likely to succeed unless it is explained to, and engages the support of, the school's own community. Vital to school success and the reduction of social class differences, therefore is community schooling — starting with teachers visiting pupils' homes at least three times a year.

Teachers need to interact with their pupils and parents in their homes. This would help to foster understanding and promote a humanistic dialogue between all concerned. Teachers, however, might be very resistant to interacting with pupils' homes. It is not clear how far this is because of the way schools are structured or because teachers have been taught to think in terms of subject 'boxes' — imparting knowledge about these rather than helping people to learn.

The issue is more than just subject-centredness against child-centredness in education; we want to get beyond this. In particular, we want to transcend the view that to be child-centred means allowing pupils to do their own thing in an unstructured situation. It doesn't — as shown by the Scope Project in Southampton.

Some maintain that social class differences may not be the main issue after all. Rather what matters is the way we approach pupils on a personal basis. We need to develop a humanistic approach to teaching and learning based on a recognition of the importance of each individual's self-perception — or self-image of his or her capacity. Others feel that personal development is an indicator of progress by which social class can also be considered, but not a replacement for it. An individualistic approach should not be set against effort to eradicate class differences but be a part of that effort.

Community education is a second recurring theme. Indeed it is more. Many problems and differences seem reconcilable by reference to a solution through local community support, understanding and participation. It is as if we must give up on change from any concerted national effort and concentrate instead on a stratetgy which we can implement and control at a local level. Giving people more control and power in education is thus a third theme: power to teachers to control the curriculum, to parents and pupils and the community over choices within and uses of the educational resources in their area, and more flexibility in schooling to aid this process in relation to individual schools.

Strong support should be given to greater pupil and student choice as well as parental choice. (But the right to 'choose' private education is not truly a right since it cannot be enjoyed by those without wealth or luck in selection. The proper word for it is privilege.)

More important still is to secure real choice within comprehensive education, putting an end to choices limited to packaged courses and giving pupils the right to discuss and decide their own programmes of learning with their teachers in the middle and later secondary years.

105

Equality means each parent and pupil with the same rights within the system rather than giving some more rights than others. People also have to be able to feel that schools are 'theirs'. To start off this process, schools must go out to people, particularly parents, and draw them into the community of the school.

The school's life has to approximate more to what life is like, operating more as a resource centre than a learning factory. It has to extend power to people to provide for themselves, to use resources for their pastimes and recreation, and for informal activity, not just for formal learning.

There are some doubts about just how far the working-class residents of any area would be more willing to become involved in a community school as against the old type of school, and whether key people are not likely always to be the middle class. But one reason to assume this may not be so is the greater working class involvement in community councils as against more traditional governing bodies and PTAs.

One hopeful development for community education so far is increased HMI involvement. But legislative support will eventually be needed: duties laid on local authorities to provide community education; standards set for each institution and the resources it requires; protection for the rights of parents to secure a broad and balanced comprehensive curriculum for their children; and a requirement — spelt out by Henry Morris as far back as 1926 — that all schools should provide leisure education and make education available for all age groups in addition to meeting the statutory educational needs of the age group designated.

Examples of work to promote community education and to narrow the social-class gap now abound.

A campus comprehensive with an on-site youth club; a crèche in operation all day; 10,000 adults on site for numerous classes; a coffee shop; the assurance to anyone who just drops in there will be someone there to chat with them; a common core for all pupils up to 16+; a staying on rate of 45 per cent into the sixth year; a community college type of governing body which has some working-class participation. More needs to be done, perhaps, to engage the support and serve the needs of local people living in council estates almost in the shadow of the campus. Sometimes they seem quite separate from all the activity.

An upper school in east London decided to end the banding system. This was a collective staff decison, made after much discussion, and promised at least to start one ball rolling. Also promising was the local authority's decision to create a new post of adviser on community education.

One school which has made a whole range of significant changes, all of which have had a positive effect. There were: (i) *Time* longer blocks for learning as opposed to short 'bits' of periods marked by bells within the delegated powers of mini-schools to plan such use of their time; (ii) *Territory* related to groups of children engaged in learning rather than groups of teachers relaying a 'subject', broadening the curriculum so that specialization is not so narrow and instituting multidisciplinary learning within mini-schools or small groups in years 1 to 3; (iii) *Teachers* broadening participation in decision-making and encouraging teacher self-development; (iv) *Things* resources for learning to be seen as a dynamic concept of resource manufacture as well as a multi-disciplinary depository serving satellite learning areas; (v) *Thinking* instituting a process of discussion and clusters of working parties which cut across the old hierarchical working of the school, giving a new role for management and the operation of the agenda for dialogue.

The widening of the 'territories' which teachers cover is one of the most crucial changes any school can now be making. But such changes have their opponents in entrenched interests such as adult education, political groups, the youth service, and teachers' professional groups, largely because the debate is conducted in institutional terms rather than in terms of viewing community education as a process at work wherever ideological learning situations are set up. Indeed some community colleges are the worst enemies of community education because of their exclusive pretentions and their occasional take-over by the middle classes.

One example though shows that such hostility is not uniform in such vested interests. It concerns a 'community committee' set up in a London institute, half of whose members are from the institute and half from the community. The invitation to representatives from all local groups to join was entirely open. Those who responded most readily were the churches, the ethnic minorities, and social action groups. The object was to let the community know what the local adult education centre had to offer in existing courses, and to ask groups if they had any educational needs they wanted the centre to meet. Several requests could be met such as help in mother tongue teaching for the women and young children of immigrant communities. Unfortunately, cuts in education have now closed down the committee since open offers of this kind can no longer be made with any assurance.

A research project in a Leicestershire community college has compared the composition of traditional local governing bodies with that of management committees of community facilities. It shows that these management committees succeed in drawing in younger people, more women, more working-class members, and people more likely to serve on this one body only and to live in the local neighbourhood. This is a factor which should be explored further.

A community school in the north operates 'unofficially' since the local authority claims to have no community schools. It is therefore run voluntarily by all the staff, teaching and non-teaching alike, along community lines. They have looked at the regulations for running schools and manage to fit in activities such as continuous opening, including weekends, cover for the activities of outside groups, use of libraries, hutted accommodation and kitchens, by constituting all activities (and their managing council) under the heading of a PTA. They have instituted changes inside the school as well, including a day-10 provision for inserting extra activity or discussion. The parents pay for a special local artist to be attached to the school. School leavers can return at any time and join any classes. Language teaching is promoted by contacts with French pupils and a French community, and by day trips to France involving residents as well as pupils.

That area has no vandalism or 'inner-city' problems, although it is by no means wealthy. Such innovations may not be possible in areas suffering from high violence levels, where schools experience unwelcome intruders, rapid depopulation, and a rundown of services. Nevertheless, reaching out could take place even if it has to be organized more specifically and overseen more carefully. It may even be more essential. Teacher willingness to volunteer time for community development without extra resources may also be unlikely in areas where social and other problems exist in great measure. Extra support would be needed.

A city community school reports it is working well with mixed ability up to 16+. Along with this goes a large staff component involved in remedial work. Efforts for change are concentrated entirely within the school's own process and its present objective is to widen the core of required work from 14 to 16 and to include more learning than that involved in English and mathematics.

An 'enabling process' is needed to encourage such developments in community schooling, plus a system of rewards for undertaking extensions of this activity.

One crucial change is in teacher education — not just for the changes discussed and advocated here, but in order to recognize the goal of 'equality of outcome' in education. Equality of opportunity is seen as no longer adequate, particularly in dealing with the gap between the social classes and what each requires — and what each gets or doesn't get — from the educational process.

Too many teachers have been sent into schools laden with early theories that the language of working class or ethnic minority pupils renders them unfit for learning in some fundamental way. This has lowered expectations for a whole generation of teachers. What is needed now is the expectation of a more positive and entirely possible new outcome.

Comprehensive education is currently being judged in a way that education was specifically advocated decades ago should no longer be judged — by the narrow test of exam results. The whole point of comprehensive reform is to go beyond such limited criteria and open up education not just to more people but to a wider definition of what education is about. It is vital we now get on with that work.

Educational Inequalities: Race and Class

Alan Little

There seem to be three reasons why school reform cannot make adults more equal. First, children seem to be far more influenced by what happens at home than by what happens in school . . . Second, reformers have very little control over those aspects of school life that affect children . . . Third, even when a school exerts an unusual influence on children, the resulting changes are not likely to persist into adulthood.

(From *Inequality* by Christopher Jencks, 1972)

I. Introduction: An Unusual Research Consensus

Recently, Mortimore and Blackstone (1982), reviewing the literature on social disadvantage and education, concluded that 'the persistence of a negative relationship between social disadvantage and educational attainment has been well documented in the research literature'. They had no doubt that certain groups (defined in terms of parental occupation, geographical location, ethnic or racial characteristics or sex) either perform less well within the school system or make the transition from compulsory to non-compulsory education less often or do not have equal access to certain types of schools, educational resources or curriculum. Further, that this negative relationship has, in their phrase 'proved to be exceedingly robust': inequalities in educational performance and participation by class, region, race and sex have persisted despite explicit policies seeking to reduce them.

The list of reports and studies that have demonstrated the relationship between parents' occupation and educational participation/ functioning is both voluminous, international and consistent. To take an extreme example, access to the final stages of education, Williamson (1981) using OECD data, calculated that the chance of a youth from the upper strata studying at a university in England and Wales in 1970 was five times greater than that of its counterpart form the lower strata: Swedish rates were much the same, in Germany the chances were twelve times as high, in the Netherlands twenty-six times, and France twenty-eight. Further, despite considerable expansion in access to higher education and explicit policies like student grants to narrow inequalities plus a wide range of pre-university educational reforms that sought to equalize opportunity, as far as the UK is concerned, there is little evidence of a sizeable narrowing of these inequalities. Halsey, Heath and Ridge (1980) estimate that the percentage of people living in England and Wales born around the first-world war (1913–22) who attended university was 1.8 per cent; for those born in the 1940s (1943/52) the percentage had increased to 8.5 per cent. Amongst those born to professional or managerial workers, the chances were eight times as great as of manual workers in the first period (7.2 per cent attending university compared with 0.9 per cent) and in the latter period, the gap had in fact marginally widened to nearly nine times (26.4 per cent compared with 3.1 per cent). This example is from higher education, similar examples could be given from the compulsory stages of education. Documentation of regional and geographical disparities is also considerable and surprisingly consistent: Richardson (1981), reviewing the international literature, argued that research yields three major conclusions:

> First, participation in higher education is greater amongst the inhabitants of metropolitan centres and large towns, and in general there is a direct relationship between community size and educational participation. Second, and a fortiori, participation in higher education is greater in urban communities than in rural ones. Third, participation in higher education is greater amongst the inhabitants of communities which have relevant institutions in their immediate vicinity.

Regional or geographical disparity exists and persists

As far as the UK is concerned, interest in racial disparities in education is comparatively recent and the literature is consequently smaller than for class or regional differences. Nonetheless, the fact of racial inequalities is well established. During the 1960s and 1970s a series of studies were completed in central London and these showed the under-functioning of children whose parents were born outside the UK (largely Caribbean and South Asian in origin). For example, of black children fully educated in the UK, instead of the expected 25 per cent in the top quartile in 'mathematics, english or verbal reasoning' at the end of primary schooling, the actual incident was 12 or 13 per cent or roughly half the expected proportion. The ILEA researchers concluded that in a cohort of London pupils tested several times during primary and secondary schooling, West Indian pupils in particular were 'reading well below the indigenous groups and that this difference cannot be entirely explained by differences in social factors or time at school in England' (Mabey, RS776/81). The overlap and interaction between class and racial or ethnic factors is important and will be returned to later: only one factual point needs to be made now. The ILEA survey compared reading ages of pupils of different ethnic origin at the age of 8, 10 and 15: at age 8, the gap between UK pupils and those of West Indian origin was ten points. When allowance was made for parental occupations, family size, parent/school contact, free meals, length of education and certain school characteristics (i.e. factors known to be associated with the educational attainment), the mean score difference fell to 4.3 points. This indicates the need to consider class and ethnic factors separately and gives some indication of the relative importance of the ethnic factor in education compared with other well-established socio-economic influences on school performance.

A note of caution must be registered here: in discussions of disparities in performance, what is being referred to are differences in relative frequencies or proportions. Although working-class children as a group do less well than middle-class, or blacks less well than whites on conventional educational measures, it should not be concluded that all disadvantaged children are doing badly (or, for that matter, all advantaged doing well) in the educational system. An illustration of this point can be obtained from the National Childrens' Bureau's research on disadvantaged children. There is no doubt that socially disadvantaged children (indicated by poor housing, low income, large families, etc.) perform less well in the school system than pupils from favoured backgrounds. Further, children who are multiply deprived (experiencing more than one disadvantage) perform less well throughout their school careers than other groups of children. Nevertheless, not all pupils who are deprived perform badly. Essen and Wedge (1983) report that 'over one-third (37 per cent) of the higher achievers were disadvantaged at the time they took their tests'. Of all 'disadvantaged' children on their definition, one quarter (26 per cent) were functioning at an above-average level for their age group.

Nevertheless, the general relationship between school functioning and social characteristics stands: in the early stages of the NCB study, Wedge and Prosser (1973) found that one in twenty of disadvantaged 11-year olds were said to be educationally subnormal compared to one in 150 of the ordinary group. Essen and Wedge (1983) report that of all the disadvantaged 5½ per cent were in ESN (M) schools at the age of 16, over nine times as many as among ordinary children (0.6 per cent). Similarly, the disadvantaged were over eight times as likely as the ordinary to be ascertained ESN (M) when they were 16, and six times as likely to have been so ascertained when they were 11. It was the long-term disadvantaged who were particularly badly off in this respect with over 12 times as many of them ascertained as ESN (M) when they were 11, and 16 times as many so ascertained when they were 16.

The same study contrasted the disadvantaged and 'ordinary' 11-year-olds and found that proportionately about five times as many ordinary children had 'good' reading ability (scores in approximately the top third of the range) and proportionately just over four times as many ordinary had 'good' maths performance. But again it is the relative frequency of 'good' performance that is being reported. The note of caution is simple, but important, not all 'disadvantaged' pupils are doing badly.

Two other findings are of immediate relevance for mapping group differences in educational functioning (especially class and ethnic inequalities). First, differences can be identified early in schooling (and often prior to school entry) and appear to widen as children progress through the system. Kellmer-Pringle, *et al* (1961) suggest that at the age of 7, over half the children with fathers who are professional/managerial workers were good readers, the percentage for the children of unskilled manual workers was less than one-quarter. A follow-up of the same birth cohort between ages 7 and 11 indicates a widening gap. Whereas the children of unskilled manual workers were 1.6 years behind non-manual workers' children at the age of 7, this had increased to three years by 11 and similar group differences were found in mathematics (Davie *et al*, 1972).

Analagous points can be made about racial inequalities. For example — there is no evidence from the ILEA material (Little, 1978), to suggest that the situation of West Indians is improving as the children progress through school. At age 8 the gap in the mean reading score between West Indians and indigenous was 10.5 standard points, at the end of primary school it was 11.2 and 15+ 12.3 points. If reading standards are an adequate indicator of skill acquisition (and there is considerable evidence to suggest that they are), one must conclude that the gap in performance is widening with school career. It is worth noting that black children are functioning at a level not only below indigenous population but also below socially disadvantaged sections of it throughout their school careers. To take one example from the same survey, at age 8+, the unskilled white worker's children had a mean reading score 4.2 points higher than their 'black' (i.e. West Indian origin), classmates fully educated in the UK; at 10+ 4.8 points, and at 15, 5.0 points higher.

II. The Social Consequences of Inequality: A Pre-disposition to Violence?

The fact of inequalities is inescapable, their persistence disturbing, and the possibility of widening differences as groups progress through the educational system, professionally worrying. It is not only that such facts highlight social injustices (see, for example, Halsey *et al*, 1980, for their implication for social mobility) but also their possible consequence for economic efficiency and social peace. Lord Scarman (1981) in his Report on the Brixton Disorders warned of the implications inequalities have for social unrest: 'the social conditions in Brixton do not provide an excuse for disorder. But the disorders cannot be fully understood unless they are seen in the context of complex political, social and economic factors which together create predisposition towards violent protest'. One of the factors he emphasized was educational opportunity and the comparative performance of disadvantaged groups within the system.

For Scarman, social inequality creates 'a predisposition towards violence and protest. Where deprivation and frustration exist on the scale to be found among the young black people of Brixton, the probability of disorder must, therefore, be strong. Moreover, many of them, it is obvious, believe with justification, that violence, though wrong, is a very effective means of protest: for, by attracting the attention of the mass media of communication, they get their message across to the people as a whole'.

III. Is It Class That Divides Us, Not Colour?

Scarman noted the shared situation of English whites and blacks in inner-city areas:

> When the young people of Brixton leave school, many of them, white and black, face unemployment. This reflects both the general economic recession from which the country is at present suffering and the contraction in the economic and industrial base of the inner city ... Many of the young people of Brixton are therefore born and raised in insecure social and economic conditions and in an impoverished physical environment. They share the desire and expectations which our materialist society encourages. At the same time, many of them fail to achieve educational success and on leaving school face the stark prospect of unemployment. Many of these difficulties face white as well as black youngsters, but it is clear that they bear particularly heavily on young blacks. In addition, young black people face the burden of discrimination, much of it hidden and some of it unconscious and intended.

He concluded: 'the black community in Brixton faces similar problems to those facing the white community, but *more severe*'.

However, it is not merely that the black condition is a more acute version of the problems facing urban working-class whites. Lord Scarman argued that for young blacks:

> Their difficulties are intensified by the sense they have of a concealed discrimination against them, particularly in relation to job opportunities and housing. Some young blacks are driven by their despair into feeling that they are rejected by the society of which they rightly believe they are members and in which they would wish to enjoy the same opportunities and to accept the same risks as everyone else. But their experience leads them to believe that their opportunities are less and their risks are greater. Young black people feel neither socially nor economically secure ... In addition, they do not feel politically secure. Their sense of rejection is not eased by the low level of black representation in our elective political institutions. Their sense of insecurity is not relieved by the liberty our law provides to those who march and demonstrate in favour of tougher immigration controls and 'repatriation' of the blacks.

Rightly or wrongly, young black people do not feel politically secure, any more than they feel economically or socially secure ... The accumulation of these anxieties and frustrations and the limited opportunities of airing their grievances at national level in British society encourage them to protest on the streets.

It is this special black dimension within the more general picture of social disadvantage and inequality that requires attention. The point is not new: for example, ten years ago the House of Commons' Select Committee on Race Relations and Immigration (1973) proposed a special Immigrant Advisory Unit within the DES to meet it. The government response (1974) was to discuss both general social disadvantage and the racial dimension, arguing that the fall in immigration will mean

an ever increasing proportion of the children of immigrant descent entering the schools will have been born in this country, many of them to parents settled here for many years or indeed themselves born here. It is true that some of these children may have been reared in the language and customs of the country of origin and may need the same sort of help as a newly-arrived immigrant child. But, where immigrants and their descendants live in the older urban and industrial areas, the majority of their children are likely to share with the indigenous children of those areas the educational disadvantages associated with an impoverished environment. The government believes that immigrant pupils will accordingly benefit increasingly from special help given to all those suffering from educational disadvantage ...

The main argument is that the needs of minorities (with the exceptions of the problems of newness, language and culture differences and discrimination) can best be met by general and radical social improvements. A further point is that policy makers are also faced by the problem of being seen to favour minority communities and ignoring the needs of the numerically larger host community especially the disadvantaged sector and therefore general programmes for social equality might be desirable politically avoiding what has been called the white backlash (Glazer, 1975).

But would they meet all the needs of the black communities? First, it must be noted that the exceptions (newness, language and culture) would still justify a serious effort if needs are to be met effectively. Secondly, the argument under-estimates the extent to which the history of racial discrimination creates problems that schools must respond to and the difficulty of creating the political climate for generating that response. Many of the difficulties facing black children are the result of long histories of colonial exploitation and the existence of colour prejudice and discrimination in contemporary Britain. Schools cannot change these things: but the educational system can try to help black pupils develop as black people in a largely white society with a sense of their own personal worth and identity. It can create additional resources and reallocate existing resources to support positive developments that will encourage the development of an educational atmosphere for both black and white pupils of mutual understanding and tolerance.

IV. Home and School: The Social Limits to Educability?

Research has not only demonstrated inequalities but also attempted to assess the relative influence of factors internal to the school and external to it on children's levels of educational success. Coleman *et al* (1966) assessed the effects of many variables on children's academic achievement in a study that included approximately 600,000 students in grades 1, 3, 6, 9 and 12 in 4000 schools. The results strongly supported two major conclusions: first, *that variations among students in levels of academic achievement are determined primarily by backgrounds* (social class), and traditional measures of the quality of a school's staff, curricula, and physical facilities account for a comparatively small amount of the differences among students; and the strong relationship between the economic and educational characteristics of families and students' levels of *academic performance increases as the children progress through elementary school*. In another publication, Coleman (1966) stated: 'The sources of inequality of educational opportunity appears to be first in the home itself and the cultural influences surrounding the home; then they lie in the schools' ineffectiveness to free achievement from the impact of the home, and in the schools' cultural homogeneity which perpetuates the social influences of the home and its environs'. Investigators in England have also compared the influence of parents and schools on the development of competence among children, and their results strongly support the conclusions stated in the Coleman Report. Douglas (1964) reported that measures of parents' interest in and involvement with their childrens' education accounted for four times as much of the variation in children's scores on intelligence and achievement tests than did measures of the quality of the schools the children attended. Similarly, the results of Moore's (1968) longitudinal study among English children indicated that these children's scores on tests of reading ability at age 7 and on tests of mental ability at age 8 were correlated with ratings of toys, books, experiences, and language stimulation provided for the children by home visitors when the children were 2½ years-old. A point that is echoed by Pollack (1972) in her study of three years in London.

The results of more recent studies also support the general conclusion that home variables are more important than school variables in determining the level of academic achievement that children attain through their studies. Mosteller and Moynihan (1972) reanalyzed the data from several large studies and concluded that variation in schools 'have little effect upon school achievement' (p. 21), and they urged consideration of methods 'to alter the way in which parents deal with their children at home' (p. 43). Jencks and others (1972) using data from several sources (including the original data collected by Coleman) contended that the most important elements in determining children's capabilities when they leave school are the capabilities and advantages that they bring to school from their homes, and that even if education could be reformed to ensure that all schools were equal in quality, inequalities in children's performance probably would continue. Finally, Coleman (1975) analyzed data from achievement tests in literature, reading, and science collected from children aged 10 to 14 years living in Chile. England, Finland, Italy, Sweden and the United States. He stated that for 'all three subjects, the total effect of home background is considerably greater than the direct effect of school variables'.

Jencks' (1972) conclusion is 'that the most important determinant of educational attainment is family background. The impact of family background is accounted for partly by measurable economic differences between families and partly by more elusive non-economic differences ... Qualitative differences between high schools seem to explain about 2 per cent of the variation in students' educational attainment ... School resources do not appear to influence students' educational attainment at all'. The educational implications of this view are only more extremely stated than the much publicized finding contained in the Plowden Report (1966) about English primary schools, that nearly half of between school reading differences are explained by a mixture of parental attitude and home circumstances, whereas only 17 per cent by factors related to the school. More recently the DES (1983) has undertaken a statistical analysis of school standards and educational expenditure: as far as public examination results were concerned as much as three-quarters of the variation between authorities can be explained by the social composition of the population, secondary school expenditure added 'a negligible further amount to this proportion'. Findings like these led Bowles and Gintis (1976) to conclude 'educational inequality is rooted in the basic institutions of our economy ... in the mutual reinforcement of class sub-cultures and social class biases in the operation of the school system itself'. In this they were echoing Jencks' (1972) assertion that the 'characteristics of a school's output depends largely on a single input, namely, the characteristics of the entering children. Everything else, the school budget, its policies, the characteristics of the teacher — is either secondary or completely irrelevant'.

VI.   What Follows: A Prescription for the System

The fact that much of the literature on educational inequalities was concerned with 'group differences' and therefore what was being described were relative frequencies of under-functioning was referred to earlier. Practitioners are not concerned with groups of pupils (black, working-class, etc.) but with individual students. This difference of viewpoint does not matter when the issues are similar to factors like the regional disparities in facilities, etc. because the solution is changing the distribution of these facilities. Nor is it crucial where the problem is to sensitize the profession to a general issue (for example, sex or racial stereotyping in school text books). However, many of the mechanisms that determine class, sex or racial disparities are not of this kind. With these what is required is the development of educationally-based strategies (given the necessary resource support) that will work in teaching situations on the social and pedagogic consequences of non-educational based inequalities. A similar point can be made about the overlap and interaction of racial and class factors. The school does not have to relate to a black child or a working-class child, but often by a child who is both black and working-class and, therefore, presents the behavioural consequences of the disadvantages that arise from social injustice. Teaching strategies must respond to the combined and reinforcing effects of both and the teacher must be sensitive to both.

The research evidence shows three main things:

(i)   that inequalities in educational functioning by class, race and sex exist and persist;

(ii) that inequalities can be identified early in schooling and appear to widen as the groups of youngsters pass through school;

(iii) that the impact of recent educational reforms on these inequalities appears to be slight.

Jencks 1972 put the point tersely when he wrote 'none of the educational evidence we reviewed can be expected to bring about significant social changes outside the schools'. Further, he concluded that the system's inability to reduce educational inequalities stemmed from three reasons: 'first, children seem to be far more influenced about what happens at home, then what happens at school ... second, the performers have very little control over those aspects of school life that affect children ... even when school exerts an unusual influence on children, the resulting changes are not likely to persist into adulthood'.

If this, in broad terms, is accepted, what are the implications for an educational strategy? Three things stand out:

(i)   the need for social policy generally to work on the social and economic roots of educational disadvantage;

(ii) the need for educational systems to find ways of working directly on the forces external to the school that influence a pupil's educational functioning;

(iii) the need for the educational system to direct more of its resources and efforts within the school to influencing the pupil's capacity to learn.

The first of these is easy to debate but difficult to implement. If low income, bad housing, poor job opportunities and other socio-economic factors are crucial influences on school functioning, then equalizing educational opportunity requires social policies that will change these things. Experience shows that efforts by the educational system and teaching profession to compensate for inequalities in living standards, employment opportunities, income differences are easier to request than implement and 'compensation' seldom works. The research evidence indicates that the task is beyond the system because these influences are too strong and too pervasive and this led Jencks (1972) to argue that the only way to achieve social equality was 'to equalize incomes'. The practical problem lies in generating a climate of opinion to support such policies. Does this mean that the educational system should simply acknowledge its inability to compete with and/or compensate for social inequalities and continue with existing practices in the knowledge that substantial groups of pupils will be underfunctioning? In my view, this is both unnecessary and unacceptable to significant sections of both the profession and the wider community. What is required are educational strategies independent of wider social reforms directed at those factors that largely determine school performance and which the school system can influence.

Three specific areas seem to be significant:

(a)   attempts to work directly with and through parents;
(b)   activities directed at student's educational motivation; and
(c)   development of structured instructional methods and teacher support.

All three can be found in the United States extension of the Head Start Programme (called *FOLLOW THROUGH*) and these are not only examples of action but all were evaluated as part of the project (W. Ray Rhine, 1982).

Parental Educational Involvement

Work at the University of Florida Institute for the Development of Human Relations, developed six styles of parental participation:

(i)   parental support in their efforts to teach their own children more effectively at home;
(ii)   parental participation as paid paraprofessionals who function as parent educators;
(iii) parental involvement in the formulation of policies and decisions on how schools should educate their children;
(iv)   parental observation of events that occur within schools, meet with school personnel and come to know them as people, and participate in a wide range of activities to acquire new information and skills;
(v)   parental participation as aides and volunteers in classrooms.

These schemes were implemented in forty-eight schools with over 7000 pupils and subjected to internal and external evaluations. The evaluation study of the Programme concluded that levels of achievement motivation 'were higher' among children enrolled in parent involvement schemes and these schemes 'produced positive results in raising the achievement levels of children'.

Behaviour Analysis Model

This work is associated with Bushell and Ramp at the University of Kansas and is concerned with motivating students, such as contingent teacher attention and praise for desirable student behaviour, token reinforcement systems, and behavioural contracts between teachers and students; individualized curriculum materials; team teaching; small-group and individualized instruction; participation by parents in classroom instruction; close monitoring of students' academic performance; and careful planning of instruction. The evaluation concluded 'that children enrolled in Behaviour Analysis classrooms achieved at or above grade level each year, with few exceptions' and 'Behaviour Analysis children scored at or above the national norm at each grade level. On the other hand, non-Follow-Through comparison children fell further below the national norm during successive years of school attendance. In fact, the comparative average reading and arithmetic scores at the end of third grade were nine months higher for students in Behaviour Analysis classrooms'. Perhaps more important was the conclusion that 'Children who attended Behaviour Analysis classrooms for the entire period of four years performed better than children who had only three years of programme experience; those who had three years of attendance had higher scores than others who had only two years; students with two years of experience performed better than those who had only one year of attendance; and children who had only one year of experience in Behaviour Analysis classrooms performed better than children who had none'.

Direct Instruction Approach

Bereiter and Engelmann are the names associated with this programme and the Model is based on the belief that children can be taught competencies more rapidly if teachers are provided with well-planned educational procedures, including pretested curriculum materials. The teachers in the Model use small-group, face-to-face methods of instruction to present carefully sequenced, daily lessons in reading, arithmetic, and language. Nearly 9000 children from low income homes participated in this programme and the evaluation found that students who attended Direct Instruction classrooms for four years, beginning in kindergarten, made substantial gains compared to the national norms on tests in reading, arithmetic, and spelling and scores among those children who entered the Model from 1969 to 1974 improved steadily year by year in reading and arithmetic and to a lesser degree in spelling.

The authors concluded that the

> evidence also supports the following summary statements: (a) The educationally significant gains that students in the model display at the end of third grade are weaker, but can still be detected, among those students when they reach fifth and sixth grade levels; (b) the teaching efforts to help low-performing children 'catch up' with their more advantaged peers are more effective when they begin at the kindergarten level; and (c) the Direct Instruction DISTAR programmes are effectively for lower-IQ students. When these findings are combined with other evidence that advantaged children gain three years in academic achievement during two years of attendance in Direct Instruction classrooms (Engelmann and Carnie, Note 9), it seems reasonable to conclude that the model can be employed to teach basis academic skills to all children.

I have listed these three examples not necessarily to recommend them but both to illustrate the three priorities I mentioned and because together they can be used to make several points about what policies work.

First, no single programme is likely to make significant inroads across the board into educational inequalities: in terms of a theory of educational functioning, it is not parental involvement or pupils motivation or structured learning programmes, but a combination of these and others. Choices might have to be made between them for resource or other reasons but in terms of our model of educational performance, all have a contribution to make but not necessarily an equal one. Secondly, impact will only be achieved if the action is sustained over time. Each part of the *FOLLOW THROUGH* evaluation emphasized the need for sustained action over long periods of the disadvantaged pupils' educational career. Programmes that are designed for only limited periods are unlikely to produce a significant influence on the pupils. Third, the indications from *FOLLOW THROUGH* evaluation are that the earlier the start of motivation programmes in a pilot development the greater the impact. Finally, programmes require the active cooperation of various groups involved professionally in education: it is not enough to leave it to the teachers, they require the support and assistance of administrators, advisors, researchers and academics, and these groups need the enthusiasm and commitment of the profession. Things that work are time consuming, involve many types of expertise, adopt a wide view of what influences a pupil's developments and are systematically thought through and planned with an explicit development, implementation and evaluation component. Needless to say, they are likely to be expensive and require the active commitment of all concerned and that could be why more schemes fail than succeed.

References

BOWLES, S. and GINTIS, H. (1976) *Schooling in Capitalist America*, London, Routledge and Kegan Paul.

COLEMAN, J. *et al* (1966) *Equality of Educational Opportunity*, Washington D.C.

COLEMAN, J. (1975) *Review of Educational Research*, 45.

DAVIE, R., BUTLER, N., and GOLDSTEIN, H. (1972) *From Birth to Seven*, Longman.

DEPARTMENT OF EDUCATION AND SCIENCE (1966) *Children and their Primary Schools* (the Plowden Report), London, HMSO.

DEPARTMENT OF EDUCATION AND SCIENCE (1974) *Educational Disadvantages and the Educational Needs of Immigrants*, Cmnd. 5270, London, HMSO.

DEPARTMENT OF EDUCATION AND SCIENCE (1983) *Statistical Bulletin 16/83: School Standards and Spending*, London, HMSO.

DOUGLAS, J.W.B. (1964) *The Home and the School*, London, MacGibbon and Kee.

ESSEN, J. and WEDGE, P. (1983) *Continuities in Childhood Disadvantage*.

GLAZER, N. (1975) *Affirmative Discrimination: Ethnic Inequality and Social Policy*.

HALSEY, A.H., HEATH A.F. and RIDGE, J.M. (1980) *Origins and Destinations*, Clarendon Press.

HOUSE OF COMMONS SELECT COMMITTEE ON RACE RELATIONS AND IMMIGRATION, (1972/73) *Education*, 1.

JENCKS, C. *et al* (1972) *Inequality: A Reassessment of the Affects of Family and Schooling in America*.

KELLMER-PRINGLE, M.L., BUTLER, N.R. and DAVIE, R. (1966) *11,000 Seven Year Olds*.

LITTLE, A.N. (1978) *Educational Policies for Multi-Racial Areas*.

MABEY, C. (1981a) *Educational Research*, 23, 2.

MABEY, C. (1981b) *Inner London Educational Authority*, RS. 776/81.

MOORE, I. (1968) *Human Development*, 11, pp. 1–24.

MORTIMORE, J. and BLACKSTONE, T. (1982) *Disadvantage and Education*, Heinemann.

MOSTELLER, F. and MOYNIHAN, D.P. (1972) *On Equality of Educational Opportunity*.

POLLACK, M. (1972) *Today's Three Year Olds in London*.

RHINE, W. R. and S. (1982) *Making Schools More Effective*.

RICHARDSON, J. (1981) *Is Higher Education Fair?*

Alan Little

SCARMAN, LORD (1981) *The Brixton Disorders*, Cmnd. 8427, London, HMSO.
WEDGE, P. and PROSSER, H. (1973) *Born to Fail?* Arrow Books.
WILLIAMSON, B. (1981) *Is Higher Education Fair?*

Language and the Education of the Working Class

Harold Rosen

As I contemplate my own title I am highly conscious of the fact that no less a person than Dell Hymes (1979) has urged us to entertain a possibility about the relationship of schools to language:

> We must consider the possibility that schools, along with other institutions, have as a latent function the maintenance and reproduction of the present social order on the apparently impartial ground of language.

'The apparently impartial ground of language' I accept must be part of my undertaking. No sooner have I said that I become aware of the risk involved in handling such weighty coinage as 'latent function' and 'reproduction of the social order'. For, whatever is said about working class children's language and what is done to it, for it and against it in schools, it is enacted in classrooms where social processes become multidimensional, spontaneous and simultaneous events (Hammersley, 1980).

I want to avoid, if possible, some of the seductions of my theme. I do not propose to be lured by it into a relatively amateurish and most certainly derivative analysis of the nature of the working class in contemporary Britain, nor into a consideration of the general issue of the education of the working class. I want as far as I am able to keep the focus on language in education. At the same time I am well aware that neither of these two issues can be ignored. I shall, therefore, state my position briefly rather than argue it.

I do so because the working class, its supposed composition and characteristics have won themselves a generous acreage of space in educational literature. Then, too, educational and sociolinguistic analysis is rarely based on a sober analysis of the realities of class in our society. We might be encouraged to expect just that when Halliday (1978) informs us that:

> The social structure is not just an ornamental background to linguistics as it has tended to become in sociolinguistic discussions. It is an essential element in the evolution of semantic systems and semantic processes.

That sounds like a promising programme. What then is this critical social structure? Schooled by Bernstein, he tells us that it is:

> ... typically the social hierachy acting through the distribution of family types having different familial role-systems.

But why should the social structure be typified by familiar role-systems? Typically I would prefer to say, the worker sells his or her labour power and arising from this primary fact the social order is adapted and shaped, an order in which, in addition to the family, there are government and its civil service, the police force, the armed forces, organized industry and commerce, the communication system and, needless to say, the educational system. I should say, in passing, that Halliday (1978) knows better than this, when he refers, for example to dialect becoming 'a means of expression of class consciousness and political awareness' though this idea is not pursued to its logical conclusion or developed.

I select Halliday as one of the most powerful sociolinguists in the Anglophone world (and perhaps beyond) who is also deeply involved in a very practical way with language in schools (see Halliday, 1981). In contrast to the family-focus of so much educational discussion of working class children, I would want quite simply to assert that those children are powerfully affected not only by the shared economic position of their parents but also by the lengthy history of education and the varied location of their parents in the social system, the different histories they inherit, their degree of class consciousness, their ethnicity and their sex. Working class children are not an undifferentiated cohort.

If we look at schools placed in the network of social relations at the intersections of specific expectations and obligations (discipline them, skill them, acculturate them, test them, certificate them, keep them off the streets) it becomes an urgent matter to consider what the possibilities are within schools for working class children. It has become commonplace of the radical critique of the schools that they are perfectly engineered institutions for reproducing the existing social order. This is supposed to hold true for the structure of the educational system, the internal organization of schools, the special version of culture they disseminate and their hidden curricula. There are other radicals who regard this critique as a betrayal of socialist endeavours to change education under capitalism. Entwistle (1981) for instance, dazzled by some of Gramsci's more dubious pronouncements, laments the abandonment of:

> Traditional socialist initiatives towards the reform of schooling aimed at creating universal access to mainstream culture.

It will be a premise of what follows that schools are neither totally efficient mechanical devices for ensuring the continuation of capitalism nor neutral purveyors of mainstream culture. If I believed the former then this present exercise would be an irrelevance. If I believed the latter, then I would be ignoring the waning of the educational optimism of the sixties and the cause for the relatively sudden interest in working class language in the sixties enshrined in that notorious dictum 'educational failure is linguistic failure'. Because schools in our society are so diverse, because they are never controlled in total fashion, because teachers themselves are not uniform, mindless zombies nor uncritical transmitters of the dominant ideology, because pupils are beginning to exert powerful pressures within the system, because politics in the community can break into sealed institutions — schools themselves are the arenas where genuine battles over contending practices are fought out. To turn our backs on them, to write them off as parts of the controlling apparatus and no more, is to refuse to participate in life itself.

With that preamble, I can now turn to what may be more narrowly construed as language issues. It feels as though it is only a short while ago that a discussion of working class children and language in school would have made obligatory an exclusive preoccupation with theories of verbal deficit and the taking of sides in the debate about Bernstein's restricted and elaborated codes. That is no longer necessary for two reasons. Firstly, the two sides have become clearly demarcated. Whereas, let us say, in 1970 the theory of codes or some now repudiated versions of it held sway, there has appeared since then a sequence of critiques which lay bare the areas of disagreement. Notably Dittmar (1976) and Edwards (1976) and most sociolinguists. Only recently there was published *Verbal Deficit: A Critique* by Gordon (1981) which not only brings together and synthesizes the ideas of the anti-Bernstein school but also traces the history of verbal deficit theory and adds its own arguments. It is no longer possible with any intellectual honesty to treat elaborated and restricted codes as though we were dealing with uncontentious objective aspects of language use. As long ago as 1963 the Newsom Report was able to present its own crass and scandalous version of verbal deficit:

> There is a gulf between those who have, and the many who have not, sufficient command of words to be able to listen and discuss rationally; to express ideas and feelings clearly; and *even to have any ideas at all.* (my emphasis)

The origin of these extraordinary assertions is made clear when the report refers to 'the evidence of research' as showing that these many idea-less have-nots have forms of speech which are restricted. The authors of the Bullock Report, who were well-placed to know about the serious criticisms of the verbal deficit thesis, simply accepted it and dismissed Labov with a condescending nod. Their way of putting it was:

> There is an indisputable gap between the language experiences some families provide and the linguistic demands of school education.

They left in no doubt who was expected to jump the gap. The careful documentation in the HMI's survey of the empty drudgery which constituted the typical linguistic demands of a school scarcely makes the educational leap across the gap seem a feat worth undertaking. As for concepts of verbal deficit (some adherents of the theory of codes, including Halliday, claim that it is not a deficit theory though how this can be true when it rests on a demonstration of what some children do not possess remains a mystery to me) they continue to exert an influence both through further refinement and dissemination (see for example Open University, 1981). But the notions of verbal deficit are there for all to see.

My second reason for not wishing to go over that ground again is that the intensity of focus on that issue alone has distracted attention from other matters and narrowed down the discussion of language and class in education.

It is a limitation in much of the literature on language and class that the language (or sociolect) of each class is treated as though it exists in isolation from that of other classes and independent of class rela-tionships. In fact it is an important feature of our society that workers encounter the language of other social strata in certain significant contexts — in their place of work, in the media, in their necessary negotiations with bureaucracy. Children encounter a sociolect different from their own in school though that contact is full of social and linguistic ambiguities. But as Edward Thompson (1963) says:

> We cannot have two distinct classes, each with its independent being. We cannot have love without lovers, nor deference without squires and labourers.

It does not take children very long to discover that their speech is disapproved of, if not actually despized, and to perceive that these criticisms come from above. In most schools for most of the time there is continuous pressure on them to use what Labov called careful rather than spontaneous speech. What this amounts to is nothing less than a drastic reduction in the linguistic resources they can call upon to express their own ideas and opinions and to come to grips with the intellectual demands made upon them. On the other hand, for older pupils in particular, it means that it is in school where the lesson is learnt that their language can be used as an oppositional weapon, the most striking example of which is the adoption by West Indian pupils of Black English *as a second dialect*. The dialect of the pupils and the dialect of the teacher do not glare at each other over the barricades. It is rather that the pupils are expected to express novel meanings when the very language in which they could best negotiate those meanings is, for the most part covertly, ruled out or attenuated. Thus legitimizing the language of working class children and more importantly, creating the conditions for its spontaneous use, become an important matter for contention.

Noel Bisseret (1970) has argued that language practices are not only a fundamental part of class identity (the nuances and ambivalence behind the phrase 'talking posh' would be a highly concentrated example) but also that the dominant ideology attempts to win, and largely succeeds in winning, acceptance of the idea that the language of the dominant is in some state of perfection and that any difference of system of meaning in the working class is only seen as an absence of meaning. The argument is complex but suffice it to say that it is not difficult to find examples of what she means. Olson (1977), in a well-known paper *From Utterance to Text* which contrasts the power of vernacular speech with the power of the written word claims that the essay-form is the ultimate high cognitive achievement of Western civilization. Dell Hymes (1979), on the other hand, attacks some of the language ideals adopted by our dominant culture:

> For a time the pinnacle of knowledge appeared to many to be a single logical language to which all science and legitimate knowledge might be reduced.

In discussing what he calls 'admissible styles' he draws attention to the undervaluing of the interpersonal, expressive, uses of language:

> Increasingly, we are concerned to have a place for things that cannot be said without distortion, or even said at all, in the idioms of elaborated, formal, purportedly rational and referential speech ... There are things we know and need to be that have no standing there. A sense of this is a reflection of the central problem of the role of language in modern society, namely what the balance is to be between modes of use of language.

So it comes about that the entrance money to be paid for advancement in the educational system creates a sharp dilemma for working class children. They may accept rhe class-based judgment passed on their language and strive to adapt and adopt the meaning system which school presses upon them. If they do so, they sever themselves from their own meaning system or even develop a contempt for it. If they reject the language the school offers they retain the class identifying power of their own but lose the opportunity of mastering much of the understanding which enables them more effectively to change their condition. The dilemma becomes the more painful when we remember that there exists in the working class both an awed reverence for the language of the educated and a deep and justified suspicion that it is used to mystify and exploit them especially in its written form — laws, contracts, missives from employers and landlords, communications from the government and local authorities etc. It requires no allegiance to the concept of hegemony to appreciate that educated language, even when delivering potent meanings, has its own pathology which derives from the social relations of communicator and audience.

In general, the language of members of the dominating class and its agents may appear *in all respects* superior, especially to themselves, solely by virtue of its dominance. It is an additional and significant step when measures are taken actively and specifically against the language of the dominated. Teachers and pupils alike are caught in an intricate knot of power relationships but they need not merely register those relationships. The Bullock Report (1975) may with apparent innocence speak of the 'linguistic demands' of the schools but this conceals both the oppresive linguistic policy of many schools and at the same time the determined efforts of many teachers that the language of working class children shall not be put down. One reason why we should be grateful for the presence of West Indian pupils in our schools is that they have brought this issue to a head.

If the phrase the 'linguistic demands of the school' means anything, it means the acquisition of standard English which is firmly counter-posed to dialect. Indeed, the Bullock Report made this very clear when it spoke of 'assisting children to master standard English which is in effect the dialect of the school'. The issues of standard English and dialect becomes one of major emphasis in language policy. Linguists have not been reluctant to enter the fray, lending their academic authority to very familiar pronouncements which are political and social rather than linguistic. Thus Crystal (1976):

> We have to be realistic. Whatever we think of the ideal of total dialect or stylistic tolerance, in all circumstances it is a present and in the foreseeable future only an ideal. The children being taught now are having to grow up in a society where the formal standard language, in its various varieties, retains considerable prestige.

And the role of the teacher is to provide the child 'with as much command of the standard form of language as possible'. There is nothing linguistic in this argument and Crystal has no privileged right to lay down the law. His views are no more cogent than the familiar common-sense ones like 'You can't change human nature' and 'Don't bang your head against a brick wall'. However, notice how surreptitiously 'standard' has become '*formal* standard' and its acquisition by working class pupils amounts to 'as much command as possible'. As in most discussion certain critical aspects of standard and dialect remain unexplored. Firstly, it is always necessary to distinguish between written standard and spoken standard and their distinct social roles. Secondly, the mistaken impression is given that standard of either modality is so tightly uniform that it does not include a very wide range of variety within itself, including its degree of closeness to spoken forms which can include an incorporation of dialect. Thirdly, and it is here where the most confusion occurs, it is the mastery of a written *system* not of written standard which is the crucial attainment. That it happens to be in standard does not mean its central characteristics derive from standard. The major difficulty for children consists in learning a form of the language which has developed its own cognitive and aesthetic strategies. To write a novel means centrally to know and understand what novels are and could be, and only in trivial sense (if at all) to know how to write standard English. And the same is true of sustained written argument and exposition. Even spelling and punctuation are requirements of a written system rather than of standard. The main problem for working class children is not that their writing is non-standard but that they have not acquired the idiom and cadences of written language and the historically developed devices for coping with and compensating for loss of face-to-face interaction. My colleague, Tony Burgess, has been observing how many working class children reach a plateau where for the most part they have acquired written standard but are only minimally at home with the written system. It has not become a genuine medium for expression.

It must be said that most linguists, at least those who concern themselves with language variety, espouse a very liberal doctrine towards dialect and this (where it has been able to penetrate) has had considerable influence among teachers. Trudgill (1975) in this country is an outstanding example. He, like others, has called down upon himself the wrath of all those who cannot perceive dialect speech as anything other than the debased, deformed lingo of the ignorant. Urban dialect, in particular, is seen as a failed attempt to speak standard. And to class bias we must add racist bias when Creole is the focus of attention. The linguists have been at pains to show since they proscribed the label of 'sub-standard', that all dialects are equal, that the vernacular speech of every society or social group is a full language in the sense that it has ordered phonology, syntax, lexis and limitless meaning potential. This point of view, which we might call egalitarian dialectology, commendably democratic though it is, leaves out what dialect means to the dialect user for whom it cannot be equal to other dialects. It has been the tradition of dialect study to note certain differences in structures, sounds and vocabulary but differences are more profound than that: they relate to ways of speaking, ways of conversing, shared idiom and shared verbal culture. This is just as true of urban dialects like Cockney, Scouse, Geordie etc., as of rural dialects.

I would like briefly to expand on that. The standard spoken dialect is a far from clearly designated territory. Whereas much ink has been spilled over the absence of the copula in Creole it is not often noticed that in standard it is perfectly possible to say 'That your car?' or 'She your sister?'. Nevertheless, since it is often referred to as the prestige

dialect or the language of the dominant we need to examine it mo
closely. Whereas it is the language of the dominant culture it is fo.
obvious reasons also the language of a huge support army of the system
which in order to carry out its duties needs also to be highly literate —
clerical and administrative workers of all kinds and, of course, teachers.
Unlike the speakers of other dialects the labour power they sell to their
employers includes the ability to speak standard and write it. These
mostly monodialectal speakers act as a kind of linguistic buffer state
between the working class and the ruling class; at the frontier of this
buffer-state inter-dialect communications are most dense. It is character-
istic of these speakers of standard to patrol their linguistic borders with
anxious surveillance to mark themselves from the working class. Thus
the prestige dialect for many of its speakers produces an anxious
monitoring of their own speech and a powerful urge to put conformity
before all else. This is all well documented in Labov (1972) who shows
lower middle class speakers to be highest on his index of linguistic
anxiety. Many, but, thank goodness not all, teachers are prey to these
very anxieties. Thus in schools there is so much obsession with certain
markers of class dialect.

Non-standard dialect speech is essentially part of an oral culture.
However, most of its speakers are consumers of standard not producers
of it; they read it but very rarely write it. The most important and
intimate exchanges of their lives are conducted through their vernacular. Perhaps, we should say that it is as dialect speakers they come
closest to being free negotiators of meaning. Oral cultures are always
rich with their own stories, jokes and songs. Most dialect speakers
operate on a continuum and it might be supposed that the powerful pull
of standard is the only dynamic force at work. why then do 'low-
prestige' varieties persist especially as there is strong research evidence
to show that speakers of low prestige varieties rate their own speech as
inferior, even unintelligent (Lambert, 1972). Against this there is the
work of Giles and his colleagues (Giles, 1975). In resisting the treatment
of a speaker as a 'sociolinguistic automaton' they assert that moods,
feelings and loyalties figure prominently as influences on people's
language. Very briefly stated their ideas are simple in the extreme.
When two people talk there is a tendency for their speech to converge
on several dimensions (speech rate, volume etc). But this only holds
true in symmetrical cooperative exchange. Where there is hostility and
conflict, speakers will diverge. This work suggests that where a group
or class identity is threatened in interaction then solidarity will lead to a
defence of the speech which identifies the group. Once again there

could be no better example of this process at work than the use of a creole by black Londoners. It is the more remarkable in that it is a variety which attracts more stigma than any other dialect both from outside and inside the speech community which uses it. The very act of speaking a dialect can be a way of saying something. In James Baldwin's words (1979):

> People evolve a language in order to describe and thus control their circumstances, or in order not to be submerged by a reality that they cannot articulate. (And if they cannot articulate it, they *are* submerged.)

We can now turn to the educational aspect of spoken language. It has been demonstrated again and again that the classroom paradigm is one which departs radically from extra-school interaction. The teacher speaks for most of the time, controls who may speak and what they may speak and channels all utterances through his or her control. In this way the verbal resources for learning become attenuated and stylized. The work of Barnes (1976) and others has shown how the verbal resources for learning can be released more effectively in groups of pupils working without the teacher. The substance of the claim has rested on verbal interaction as a powerful learning medium. It is necessary in the light of what I have been saying about working class speech to add that the claim becomes more telling since it is only in small group interaction that spontaneous vernacular speech can be realized in classroom conditions. I cannot develop the argument fully here but only want to point to the fact that the growing body of work on classroom interaction has not to my knowledge given any attention to this matter. We might add improvized drama to take the discussion still further. And to add the oral culture of the pupils is to go further still. Some groups of teachers have already done so (Rosen, 1978).

I want now to return to the question of literacy. As we have seen, the issue of standard is something of a diversion. However, with certain significant exceptions, the printed language in our culture is standard and has been for a long time in spite of Burns and the nineteenth-century Lancashire poets. Literacy exists as two complementary activities but from the point of view of the learner, especially the working class child, they are two distinct activities. Reading obliges *all of us* to enter a world which is different from our speech. It is there for the meaning to be extracted. Writing demands that we make the meaning. This involves either censoring out or adapting spoken forms. Allowing for this universal difficulty facing all children, there may well be special difficulties for working class children.

First, there is the question of linguistic distance. The standard-speaking child is in many respects closer to the written form especially that which he finds in most primers. This may not be critical but it might be more critical for some dialects than others since the linguistic distance might be greater. But there is another aspect to this which has not to my knowledge been fully explored. The standard speaking child experiences receptive literacy before he/she starts to learn to read and write. His/her parents are more likely to be literacy saturated and consequently literacy feeds back into their speech. It is an interesting question in its own right to consider not only what literacy does to our consciousness but also what it does to our everyday speech. It is possible that some children do get a flying start in learning to read for those reasons. But that is merely speculative. What is certain is that literacy almost by itself is at the centre of current controversy in education. Many critical questions are brushed aside as it takes the centre of the stage. And the notorious fact is paraded again and again that it is above all working class children who fail at reading and writing. Usually it is reading rather than writing which is placed at the centre for there is much more concern about the ability to receive messages than to deliver them. We should never forget that most working class children do learn to read and write (as any tube journey would show us). Nevertheless, it should be a concern that many do not or do so at such a low level that there is justified concern about is having more than minimal effectiveness. It has been suggested (Postman, 1973) that reading for working class children is so organized that it ensures that they become obedient citizens but of course there is no shortage of reading which does something very different or even would make them disobedient citizens. There may be all sorts of conflicting motives for wanting to teach children to read but I am in no doubt that working class children have particular cause to need literacy. They need it so that they shall not be manipulated by the printed word; they need it so that they become confident users of the written language for their own purposes; they need it so that they can seek out those books and writings which best speak to their experience and aspirations. Paul Willis (1977) in spite of his devastatingly critical analysis of how schools fail working class children concludes that:

> ... it is a condition for working class development that working class kids do develop certain disciplined skills in expression and symbolic manipulation.

There can be no single explanation for reading failure but it is imperative that we look for ways to eliminate failure amongst working class children. We have some clear pointers.

(i) Dialect is not a barrier in learning to read as Goodman (1973) demonstrated so clearly:

> The only disadvantage which speakers of low-status dialects suffer in learning to read is imposed by teachers and schools. Rejection of their dialects and educators' confusion of linguistic differences with linguistic deficiency interferes with the natural process by which language is acquired and undermines the linguistic confidence of divergent speakers.

(ii) Labov suggests that failure in reading was not a rejection of literacy but a rejection of the school culture in which reading (we could add, conceived of in a particular way) played a central and symbolic role.

(iii) The healthiest sign we have had is the involvement of working class parents in the teaching of reading including the making of books. This entry into schools could have much deeper and richer consequences for the schooling of their children. It also cuts through the mystique of the reading industry.

But to launch children into literacy is only the beginning of the process which could make them into confident, critical readers and powerful effective writers. For this to happen the whole context of the use of language must be one which confirms and extends their experience, which makes room for their ways of speaking. And that is a long way from what we have in the past conceived of the well-ordered school dispensing a certain kind of nerveless language, free from risks and obsessed with proprieties.

I have not forgotten Dell Hymes' warning with which I began 'the maintenance and reproduction of the present social order on the apparently impartial grounds of language'. We have to unveil the impartiality of language not only for ourselves but also for our pupils. This can mean creating a language curriculum in which the mysteries of linguistic judgment are laid open to the active investigation by the pupils themselves of how language works in our society. The vacuum left by the abandonment of traditional grammar teaching can be filled by inviting working class pupils to study their own langauge, the diversity which surrounds them and the linguistic myths which have helped them to keep them in their place. Here at last we can say the work is in hand and *The Languages Book* is already in use in London schools.

I am not so blithe about our schools as to believe that major shifts can occur without struggle and with more than limited possibilities for success but where there is success, and we can point to it, it becomes more important than its limitations would suggest. For this is the way we begin to work out, not in grand schemes and dreams but in lived experience, an alternative society.

Meanwhile there is much to do. I have had no time to consider the implications of bilingualism in our schools, what it means to be a learner of English as a second language, nor huge changes we need in the literature programme. There is exciting work to be done. Consider narrative in the widest and deepest sense of the word. What do we do with it in schools compared with its role in cognition and its pervasiveness in working class culture. Consider it as a form of explication, persuasion, and exploration of the possible.

Let me practise what I preach with a borrowed story to set all I have had to say in proportion. I borrow it from Geneva Smitherman's *Black English and the Education of Black Children and Youth* (1981). It is told by Reginald Wilson:

> I'm standing by the shores of a swiftly flowing river. I hear the cry of a drowning man. So I jump into the river, pull him to the shore and apply artifical respiration. Then just as he begins to breathe, there's another cry for help. So I jump into the river, reach him, pull him to the shore and apply artificial respiration. Then just as he begins to breathe, another cry for help. So back into the river again. Reaching, pulling, applying, breathing and then another yell. Again and again, without end goes the sequence. I'm so busy jumping in, pulling them to the shore and applying artificial respiration that I have no time to see *who is upstream pushing them in.*

Education and Social Class: Race and Language: Discussion

Society is riddled with prejudice. Individuals and whole communities are discriminated against because of their race, their sex, their class. If we are to organize learning effectively in such a society we must start by recognizing this fundamental fact — and recognize too that language carries the prejudice like a water-borne disease.

Our aim must be to value equally individual members of equally valued communities; and to find ways in which we can approach this through language.

The Recognition and Extension of Linguistic Competences

All linguistic competences must be recognized and valued. Children are talented users of language, capable of a wide range of oral discourse. Ambition is born of self-confidence. But however confident children may appear by extrovert behaviour in the classroom, they are often very unconfident about expressing themselves in teacher-defined contexts. We must, therefore, encourage them to use their language freely and unselfconsciously in such situations as an essential first step towards extending their competence. We can do that best by respecting their talent, and showing we place a high value on it.

Teachers must beware of making assumptions about the limitations of children's linguistic competence. Children often choose not to engage in a teacher-defined context. Such assumptions often lead teachers to have expectations that are too low. Both pupil and teacher have a well-documented tendency to fulfil the prophecies each makes about the other.

Schools tend to define too narrowly what are acceptable subjects of study and types of discourse. Barriers are often created for many children by a teacher's treatment of a subject which is alien to them and employing language and written sources that are almost unintelligible. Schools have to value what interests children, and the language in which they choose to express that interest (remember *Kes*), in order to encourage them towards what interests schools and the kind of written language with which schools choose to measure ability.

Schools should find ways to extend the range of children's linguistic competence and skills to give them power and status in the school community. Children must have experience of the language of discussion, argument, assertion, petition, questionnaire, agenda and minutes. Schools should take notice of and act upon their opinion. Only by giving responsibility to children will they themselves take responsibility for the work and behaviour of themselves and those around them.

We must examine how children see the language used in the school to articulate significant things. Schools should look at the public statements — spoken and printed — which define a school's stance on anti-sexism, anti-racism, whole school policies, respect for other people's languages and cultures. Teachers should understand and accept their responsibility as articulators of the school's values.

References to 'standard English' — often in the context of deploring children's failure to speak or write it efficiently — are really statements about social class by teachers who know little about language beyond what they themselves have been taught to be acceptable forms of spoken or written expression. Linguists confirm that standard spoken English is rich and varied in the number of words, phrases and grammatical utterances which are universally understood and accepted. The identification of class by accent or dialect is another matter. One cannot deny its significance in our prejudice-ridden society, but one should never confuse it with notions of correctness.

Language and Learning

A language policy across the curriculum is essential. We must make space in all subjects for the analysis of language needed for learning. All teachers are teachers of language and it is vital for a school to have common policies for teacher response to talk and to writing.

Constructing written discourse is a problem for everyone. Few people — even teachers — feel confident about constructing a piece of written language in an appropriate register to have the desired effect on the intended audience. Teachers often fail to realize how sophisticated and difficult a task it can be for many pupils.

The active and imaginative exploration of language by children is essential to their learning. Thought and language are bound together in a symbiotic relationship that borders on synonymity. 'How do I know what I think until I see what I say?' is a question that brings us close to the creative processes of learning.

The different value placed on types of spoken and written language should be challenged. Pupils tend to be measured not on their grasp of the fundamental ideas of a subject but rather on their ability to describe those ideas in middle-class English prose with prescriptive overlays according to the exigencies of particular disciplines. The testing of a hypothesis in history, geography, English literature or science in the same week of 'O' level written papers presents pupils with different challenges, many of them entirely linguistic. This is an unacceptably narrow way of judging pupils' abilities. The testing of learning should not depend so completely on levels of competence in standard English written forms.

There must be space and time for small group discussion of prejudice — racism, sexism, ageism and class. Talk is vital and everyone must speak.

Small group work of any kind builds confidence towards participation in larger forums, just as personal language work of any kind builds confidence towards competence in impersonal, transactional discourse.

There should be support for bilingual pupils specifically within mainstream learning. Schools should not disseminate resources for ESL support generally through the school. Local authorities should satisfy themselves that such resources are identifiable and used for their right purpose. The range of ESL need — from those pupils with no English to those who function well — should be more widely recognized in schools and strategies should be developed which are more sensitive to the different levels of need.

Greater consideration should be given to the most effective ways of teaching learning skills. Literacy skills are indivisible and best learned by active participation — listening and talking, reading and writing.

The Languages Curriculum

Learning *about* language should be a fundamental part of the curriculum.

Community languages must be recognized and given status throughout the life of the school — displays, teachers knowing words and phrases of greeting and praise in the main language spoken at home by bilingual pupils, availability of interpreters, the translation of letters and documents, and so on. Secondary schools can learn much from good primary school practice.

We must give more consideration to the message given out by a school which studies only European languages. All schools in multicultural areas should provide access to as many non-European languages as possible — and at least one where numbers do not permit more.

Community languages and dialects should be given proper status in school. There is a lot of ground to be made up here as generations of parents have suffered a sense of inferiority in school every time they opened their mouths — which is why so many of them never do.

The Organization and Structure of the School

Schools should set up explicit central structures to combat prejudice and to encourage good practice. Responsibilities should be evident in the staffing structure and a detailed description of each responsibility holder's tasks in the school staff handbook. Named people in school departments should ensure school practices are free from such prejudices. The timetable should also reflect good practice, such as mother tongue teaching, ESL support, continuity and stability of the learning environment.

Staff should know how structures work and why things are organized as they are so that even when conditions change — falling rolls, amalgamations, cuts in resources — the organization can respond to change and still keep its anti-prejudice structures intact.

School structures for policy-making and evaluation should involve pupils, parents and governors as well as teachers. For example developing a whole school policy against racism is a process which should involve all sections of a school community. Such processes, once developed, can profitably be extended to areas of policy-making and evaluation which have traditionally been the prerogative of teachers alone.

Alternative structures for learning should be available in schools to allow more negotiation, more flexible use of time, and more genuine choice. 'Alternative' days or weeks on the Stantonbury Campus model and mini-schools are recommended as examples of the directions schools could be taking. Links with colleges, work and community service, residential experience, are all ways of broadening the base of learning and making the learning experiences more effective.

School and Community

We must value children not only as individuals but as members of social classes and ethnic groups. Teachers must care more about the communities they work in.

Multiculturalism and anti-racism are matters for the whole school community actively to involve itself in. Similarly communities should be encouraged to participate in the life of the local school. We should use opportunities of community concern to unite school and community. Schools should allow significant amounts of time for meeting individual parents and use community languages in written communication.

Schools should strive to ensure that all appropriate communities are represented on teaching and non-teaching staffs and that there are ethnic minority holders of some senior posts. We must recognize and deal with the often unconscious racism and apathy whenever we meet it on school staffs, in governing bodies, among groups of parents or pupils, or in ourselves. Schools must recognize and understand cultural and community customs — for example, the use of black British dialects to express identity and solidarity; religious food laws; who may accompany a female pupil home late at night after a school outing. Such customs can cause problems and only by understanding the custom can schools better help and understand the pupil.

We must learn to define success not only in the narrow terms of an acquisitive society but in the broader terms of equipping children for self-fulfilment, with the desire and skills to change society for the better.

Schools must be aware of pressure to depoliticize and thus emasculate the curriculum. To organize learning is a political act. In many contexts encouraging children to think, to question, to challenge and to consider alternatives to the status quo can be regarded as subversive by a ruling political party. Such attempts to control and thereby impoverish learning must be resisted if we are to achieve the aim of valuing equally individual members of equally valued communities.

Jobs and Careers: Class, Schools and the New Vocationalism

Sue Holmes and Ian Jamieson

Introduction

Since the early 1970s work opportunities have collapsed at a pace not seen since the 1930s. The expectations of young people, that they would enter work on leaving school, have collapsed with them. If one of the aims of secondary schooling is to prepare young people for adult life it might be expected that changed expectations would have resulted in a fundamental reappraisal of the curriculum. This chapter suggests that this has not occurred and identifies reasons for the lack of response. It outlines the frustation felt by other state institutions, and particularly the Manpower Services Commission, with the schools' inability to make what they consider to be appropriate changes. This has resulted in a series of initiatives from outside the education system which 'encourage' the schools to make changes and remove their school leavers for training rather than work.

Unemployment

The period from the end of the Second World War until the early 1970s was one of continuously high employment. Young people could expect to find a job on completion of their full-time education and, since a higher proportion of children from the professional and managerial classes went to grammar school and university than from the manual worker classes, the strong correlation between social class and occupation continued. The dramatic changes in the structure of the job market since the early 1970s have meant that increasing numbers of young people have not found jobs on completing their schooling, and the process of moving from school into work is a hazardous, lengthy and debilitating process for many young people.

For how long will this situation continue? Several factors have contributed to the decline in job opportunities on a scale not seen since the 1930s. The population of working age is continuing to increase. Between 1979 and 1981 earlier retirement by men and a decline in the numbers of women moving into employment created some reductions in the labour force (i.e. those available for work); but this was offset by increases in population so that the total available labour force increased by one quarter of a million. Current projections anticipate a further increase in the available labour force of one quarter of a million by 1986. Despite this, those actually employed fell by over one million from 1978 to 1981. Such a sustained fall in the availability of jobs is without precedent in the post war period. Perhaps the most important contributory factor was the ferocity of the recession (Metcalfe and Richardson, 1982).

Youth Unemployment

At a time of falling employment prospects the young who have not yet entered the labour market are at a particular disadvantage, since employees tend to hold on to their jobs and employers fail to recruit, or employ the ready trained and skilled. This fall in job opportunities seems to affect all young people entering the labour market, although the well-qualified are less likely to be unemployed or made redundant.

Table 1: Qualification in relation to economic activity and age: GB 1981

Age 16–29 Male	Unemployment rate %
First or higher degree	6.7
Trade apprenticeship	10.8
'A' level	10.9
'O' level	14.7
CSE	18.4
None	27.0

Source: Employment Gazette, April 1983.

It has been estimated that a 1 per cent rise in male unemployment is associated with a 1.7 per cent rise in young men's umemployment, and a 1 per cent rise in female employment with a 3 per cent rise in young women's unemployment (Makeham, 1980).

Table 2: October 1981 unemployment rates by age and sex in Britain

	Under 19	18–19	20–24	25–34	35–44	45–44	55–59	60+	All
Male	6.0	9.7	19.5	22.6	15.6	13.4	9.4	3.7	100
Female	9.9	15.8	24.4	22.2	10.3	10.8	6.4	0.1	100

Source: Employment Gazette, November 1984

Young people have been disproportionately hit by job cutbacks resulting from recession, but the fall in total employment opportunities hides substantial changes in the structure of employment. From 1979–81 those actually employed fell by over one million, but manufacturing and construction industries lost over 1,200,000 jobs whilst employment in the service industries increased by 200,000. Young people traditionally enter the labour market in the non-manufacturing sector; most find jobs in distribution, construction, insurance, banking and finance. Jobs in these sectors, with the exception of construction, have not disappeared so rapidly as in manufacturing; but new job opportunities have not been created. The decline in manufacturing has brought cuts in the more attractive job opportunities, for example, craft apprenticeships. Labour market predictions are for a continuous decline in numbers employed in craft operations.

Unemployment and Socio-Economic Groups

Another aspect of the continuous and dramatic decline in manufacturing industry is the decline in work opportunities for the unskilled, and the young unskilled about to enter the job market are particularly disadvantaged. The following table indicates the proportion of the labour force in each socio-economic group which enters the unemployment register each month: it shows clearly the risks of unemployment attached to being unskilled in the labour market.

In 1977 the MSC's Working Party on Young People and Work found that unemployed young people tended to come from the lowest social groups C2, D and E. Very large increases in the numbers of the young unemployed since this date must inevitably suggest that more social groups are feeling the effects of unemployment, but the range of statistics available viz: those on page 148 which show the high proportion of the unskilled entering the unemployment register, and DES statistics (Statistical Bulletin 12/83) which continue to show participation in 16+ education being strongly related to social class,

Table 3: Monthly male unemployment inflow rates by socio-economic group in autumn 1978

Socio-economic group	monthly inflow rate (%)
Senior and intermediate non-manual	0.4
Junior non-manual	0.9
Foremen and skilled manual	0.9
Semi-skilled manual	1.4
Unskilled manual	4.4
Personal service, for example, waiters, bartenders.	8.4
Miscellaneous occupations, for example, farmers, farmworkers, own account workers	0.7
All identified	1.0

Source: Employment Gazette, January 1983.

suggest that those young people from the families of the semi-skilled and unskilled tend to suffer disproportionately.

Unemployment by Sex, Ethnic Origin and Region

National employment statistics tend to overlook very considerable differences in work opportunities for different ethnic groups and young people in different areas of the country. A survey by the Commission for Racial Equality in 1982 found that amongst young whites and Asians in inner city areas, out of every ten in the potential work force, six were in work and four were unemployed. Asians were more likely to continue at school or college than whites, but how far this is related to greater difficulty in finding work is difficult to estimate. For the Afro-Caribbean the picture is gloomier. For every ten available for work, four were in work and six were unemployed. Local labour markets may mean that young people in certain towns and cities face disproportionate risks of unemployment. There are marked regional variations in the unemployment figures, with areas like the West Midlands, Wales and the North East particularly badly hit. But even in the relatively better off areas like the South East, there are still sinks of unemployment like inner London.

The evidence relating unemployment to sex differences is complex. Women have entered the labour force in increasing numbers since the Second World War, and three out of four women work in the service industries which have fared better than manufacturing in the depression. On the other hand, the pattern of female employment is not the same as that for men. There are, for example, far more women in part-time jobs. Amongst school-leavers there is still more female unemployment, but the evidence from the DES Statistical Bulletin (DES, 1983) suggests that girls are more likely than boys to go back to school if they cannot get a job.

Technological Change

Are these changes permanent? Those who are involved in devizing policies for the unemployed and those entering the labour market need to look not only at current trends but also at predictions for the future. Government, and particularly the MSC, are convinced that unemployment rates will fall when the upturn in the economy arrives. This chapter has argued that whereas youth employment is being particularly hard hit by cyclical unemployment, long-term changes in the structure of the economy might result in historically high levels of unemployment for many years to come. There are those who argue that technological change is bringing about continual changes in the structure of employment which makes large-scale unemployment inevitable, but the impact of technology on jobs is very difficult to predict. The optimists suggest that technology will catalyze structural change and that unemployment will only rise during the difficult transition period: more jobs will be available in the industries which produce components, and the wealth produced by the service industries will lead to new employment opportunities. The pessimists point to the capital intensive nature of production and its demand for a smaller skilled workforce. They see the unskilled as being particularly at risk.

Self Employment

Other commentators see the regeneration of employment through self employment. In fact, the role of self employment in the economy declined until recently. In 1921, 10 per cent of the employed worked for themselves, but by 1981 the figure had fallen to 9 per cent. There has been a large increase in registration of new firms since 1972, but there must be considerable doubt about the amount of employment which can be created in this way. The data that we have suggests that young people under the age of 25 run particularly high risks of failure in starting up their own businesses, (Bourne and Gould, 1983). The policies currently being posited to encourage small enterprises affect only a small proportion of productive activity: the employment policies of large enterprises, which employ a large proportion of the working population, are still major determinants of total employment (Census of Production, 1978). More worrying is the sharp fall in tax revenue from small firms which the Inland Revenue noted between 1972 and 1976. Does this indicate that, despite an increase in the number of small businesses, their ability to succeed falls dramatically during recession?

The Informal Economy

Unemployment figures mask those who are gainfully employed but do not register this i.e. those working in the 'informal economy'. OECD estimate that the size of the informal economy may be larger than originally thought, although the variation in the scale of estimates (involving 3 per cent to 35 per cent of the nation's labour force) makes guesstimating hazardous. Evidence from the UK suggests that the informal economy is at its peak when the economy is in full boom or full recession (Smith, 1981). At times of recession more people are forced to take 'marginal' jobs, with low wage levels and poor working conditions offered by employers faced with uncertain markets and high wage levels; and also to look for job opportunities in the community. These tend to be mundane, unskilled tasks — construction, home maintenance, gardening, leisure, catering, domestic work, etc. Housewives, pensioners and students are thought to form the core of this band of disguised workers. For those on the unemployment register this work would not be seen as an appropriate substitute for 'real work', although it may make an important contribution when family income is falling.

Responses to Economic Change

The economic problems of Great Britain have resulted in a long debate about social structures. This may be seen as part of a continuing debate which has risen to a crescendo at times of economic crisis, as in the 1920s and 1930s. As Britain's economic problems rapidly increased with the international oil crisis of 1973/74, the notion that the nation would gradually grow richer, and release more funds for state services such as education, disappeared. In the late 1960s the Black Papers had claimed that standards were falling and that a policy of social engineering through education was doomed to failure. The increasing level of youth unemployment served to intensify the debate about the role and nature of secondary education in the UK. Now, education was seen as contributing to the economic crisis by discouraging pupils, and particularly able pupils from looking favourably on industry as a career and also by failing to prepare young people for work. Callaghan's speech at Ruskin College in October 1976 did not initiate a Great Debate, it merely gave dignity to the claims of educational shortcomings which were being voiced at this time.

What is most remarkable about the debates stemming from the changed economic situation was the lack of attention given to the underlying reasons for Britain's decline, an approach so necessary to put the discussion about the role of education into some perspective. The emphasis which was placed on secondary education's role in preparing a suitable workforce, when the lack of training opportunities for young workers in specific occupations was largely ignored, was reprehensible. European comparisons show how small is Britain's commitment to systematic formal, vocational preparation. The NIESR Economic Review 1981 suggested that two-thirds of the British workforce had no vocational training at all compared with one-third of the workforce in West Germany, and that the training of those, predominantly working class, who did not seek traditional academic routes into work was largely neglected.

Economic changes and the debate which they engendered had their effect. The polity made a diagnosis and decided to act. Significantly, its main agency has been a non traditional body, the Manpower Services Commission. In 1974 the MSC extended its brief to look at the adequacy and relevance of all forms of education and training received by young people prior to or on entering work. Its immediate task was to look at the problems of the young unemployed. A large range of schemes was established, so that from 1974 until 1982 for ever increasing numbers of school leavers there were no jobs or careers but only 'opportunities' as more and more young people found themselves on youth opportunities programmes (YOP). These one-year programmes took 162,2000 young people (1978/79) and expanded to 553,000 (1981/82). They were explicitly and by implication directed to young people with few or no educational qualifications, amongst whom it was considered the unemployed were concentrated. The programmes aimed to enhance the employment prospects and the pastoral, social and educational development of young people. There was often the implication that schools had failed them.

A study of YOP trainees in Leeds (Banks, Mullings and Jackson, 1983) who were 1979 school leavers found that entrants to training tended to be male, West Indian and with few educational qualifications. The opportunities offered seemed to reflect training for traditional work and the traditional work patterns of the different ethnic groups. These trainees had, on the whole, been very satisfied with their training. Two years after leaving school, 36 per cent of those who had undertaken a YOP course were unemployed.

The increasing numbers of school leavers without work, and dissatisfaction with YOP resulted in the replacement of YOP. The Manpower Services Commission's own reports suggested that one-third of YOP trainees were being used as cheap, substitute labour and two-thirds received poor training. In 1983 the Youth Training Scheme was launched with the guarantee that there would be places for all 16 year olds who required them. The aim was to train a well equipped and adaptable workforce with transferable skills and enhanced personal effectiveness.

In its first year 354,000 young people joined the Youth Training Scheme (YTS). Early surveys suggest that the goal of a comprehensive training scheme was not being met. 'There is little evidence of integration or co-ordination of core skills, vocational studies and work experience across the various parts of scheme . . .' (HMI Report quoted in the *Times Educational Supplement*, 7 December 1984). A two-tier scheme is developing, with the more prestigious 'Mode A' schemes on employers' premises taking three quarters of all white trainees but only 55 per cent of trainees of African or West Indian origin, and 59 per cent of Asian trainees. There is at the time of writing no unambiguous evidence available on the destination of the first cohort of YTS trainees. There is general agreement, however, that less than 50 per cent have subsequently entered full-time employment.

The Schools

We have argued two important propositions: first, that there have been major structural changes in the British economy and that these allied to a cyclical depression have led to high levels of youth unemployment. Secondly, we have noted that with the economy in difficulties, important groups in society, including both the major political parties, have turned to the education system as part cause of the problems. How has the schools sector of the education system reacted to these twin pressures of economic and social change, and political pressure? And if schools have reacted have the changes affected all pupils similarly, or has differentiation by social class taken on new forms?

We must be clear how change occurs in schools. It is not sufficient for there to be radical changes in the socio-economic structure for schools to change. There must also be a perception on the part of those who control our schools that change has occurred and is significant for what is transacted in schools and secondly, there needs to be the view that such changes are not a temporary abberation that will pass. Finally, there needs to be either a belief amongst those in a position of influence that education in schools ought to be related to changes in socio-economic structure, *or* there needs to be a mechanism that in some way ensures a degree of congruence between the education system and the socio-economic structure. Space does not permit us to unravel the full complexity of these issues, and in particular to join in the debate with Bowles and Gintis (1976) which has so influenced recent writings in the sociology of education in this country. However, several points must be made clear; first, that there is no mechanism which automatically adjusts the education system to the needs of the economy, even supposing it was clear what the 'needs of the economy' were. Secondly, that in the devolved system of education operated in this country it becomes necessary to *convince* education authorities and schools of the need for change. It follows from this that the *perception* of changes in the outside world becomes an important factor.

The Curriculum

It will be useful to divide our remarks on the curriculum into separate sections on curriculum content, pedagogy and examination and assessment. One consequence of the devolved system of education is that it becomes very difficult to obtain reliable and systematic data about what is happening in schools. Our overall diagnosis is that a combination of massive socio-economic change in a very short period of time (particularly, high youth unemployment), exhortations from government via the DES, and a plethora of 'projects' have in fact managed to have some small effect on the school curriculum. We must stress, however, that with one or two exceptions, the effects are relatively minor. Despite the massive changes that we have outlined in the first section of this chapter, most pupils are being taught the same material, by the same methods and are being examined in the same way as they were ten years ago.

Curriculum Content

Until the last few years it has always been important in talking about secondary education in England and Wales to draw a sharp distinction between education and training. Education not training has been the business of compulsory schooling. In fact the distinction is wholly artificial, both practically and theoretically. What the divide has meant however, is that very little occupationally specific work has been transacted in schools.

A simplistic picture taken at the beginning of the 1970s might have looked like this. The needs of the white collar, managerial world were best catered for. Teachers concentrated on written work and abstract reasoning skills which were and are demanded by the professions and semi-professions. Children who did well at school in major subjects like English, history, geography, mathematics and the natural sciences progressed, often via higher education into 'middle class' jobs. As other papers in this collection have shown those children of parents who themselves had to use these skills in their jobs possessed obvious advantage over their fellow students who had not inherited such 'cultural capital' from their parents.

Many schools also tried to deliver technological and craft skills to the labour market via their pupils — particularly boys. Yet these subjects on the timetable (woodwork, metalwork, and even the 'new' subject of craft design and technology) were clearly of lower status in the school, reflecting, it might be argued, the lower status of these occupations in society.

Pedagogy

We know even less about pedagogy in our schools than we do about curriculum content. And there has been very little work done on the relationship between pedagogy and educational achievement by social class. Perhaps, the major feature to be remarked on in our 1970s snapshot is the emphasis on a didactic mode of teaching, with the teacher as the 'expert', the purveyor of knowledge. Much of this stems from the emphasis on 'facts' in the curriculum rather than skills or attitudes. What evidence we have seems to show that didactic teaching is best suited for knowledge (facts) rather than the development of skills and attitudes, and we know that by and large the higher social class tend to perform best in the 'knowledge' area. Furthermore, many of the skills necessary for *manual* jobs are best taught experientially.

Examinations and Assessments

Although previous economic crises in the 1920s and 1930s caused employers to question the outputs of the educational system and thus by implication the system of examinations, by and large employers were content to use its rough and ready system of grading. Certainly life was easier before the advent of comprehensive schools. The distinction between secondary moderns and grammars provided a rough and ready fit with the manual/non-manual occupational structure; when all the children came from one school closer attention had to be paid to examination passes. A system which was designed to produce 20 per cent with GCEs, 40 per cent with CSEs and 40 per cent with nothing, gave a crude benchmark of occupational suitability for employers which served them well enough until the 1970s.

A Diagnosis for Change

We have provided an extremely crude sketch map of the curriculum seen from an occupational point of view up to the 1970s. In short, neither the content, pedagogy nor assessment system was much in time with industrial needs but employers adapted themselves to the nature of the output produced by the system. It allowed them very approximately to slot people into the occupational hierarchy. Education had the overall effect of reinforcing the existing occupational structure — the cornerstone of social class. Working class boys and girls entered school and did poorly, they were channelled into subjects thought best suited for working class jobs, emerged with few qualifications but had little difficulty in finding jobs in manual occupations. Importantly, there were enough individual exceptions to this tendency, both in schools and industry, to prevent there being any clearly defined and widely felt social problems. There were enough working class youngsters succeeding in the educational system to safeguard the operation of the school system, and perhaps even more importantly, British industry had not reached the highly bureaucratic stage where qualifications were the only means of rising through the ranks.

By the 1970s there were a number of strains in the system. The expansion of tertiary education had meant that many able youngsters who would normally have gone into skilled manual jobs, particularly apprenticeships, were staying on in education. As a consequence, many employers were now meeting an ability range below the level they had been used to. This is the simple origin of the numeracy and literacy 'problem' that was rediscovered in the late 1960s and early 1970s. It also provided a major thrust for the 'Education isn't working' movement associated with the employers' natural political allies — the Conservative party. Confirmatory evidence for this diagnosis must surely be provided by the virtual disappearance of the numeracy and literacy lobby now that the shortage of jobs has meant that employers can once again recruit from a more able group of young people. There are specific problems that irk employers. For example, the difficulty of recruiting people with certain specific skills, initially skills relevant to the engineering industry and more recently those in computing and microelectronics. The charge was a double one. Schools didn't teach relevant subjects and skills, and furthermore transmitted an aristocratic, bookish culture which denigrated (if only by neglect) the world of trade and industry. Some interpreted the charge in class terms. On one view schools were dominated by a middle class (strictly an upper middle class) set of values and thus were failing working class youngsters; but others saw schools offering the sons and daughters of the manual classes a chance to acquire the culture and qualifications necessary to lift them out of their class of origin. For their part the schools blamed the universities for determining the curriculum via their stranglehold on the examination system, and 'society' for downgrading in status the very occupations it declared were necessary for economic survival.

Of more general and fundamental concern was not specific mismatches of qualification or skills but the problem of *attitudes*. The problem is a complex one, and it shifts over the course of time. It is obfuscated by the language chosen to describe the problem, in particular by the attempt to legitimate talk about attitudes by referring to them as skills. The initial problem could be described as an almost nineteenth-century worry about the attitudes of the labouring classes. School leavers didn't seem keen to work, lacked a pride in their job, were bad timekeepers, ill disciplined, etc., etc. Such complaints often merge into worries about the general social competence of young people. It is at this point that talk of attitudes merges quickly into talk about 'social and life skills'.

High levels of youth unemployment have not lessened these concerns. Many in government and its vigorous arm the MSC seem to be arguing, at least implicitly, that high levels of youth unemployment are caused precisely because young people have this set of attitudes. As a consequence employers prefer to retain their existing workforce or employ more 'mature' workers. In addition, there is the argument that this rather tenuous 'will to work' that the young have might be eroded entirely by long periods of unemployment. Thus one of the major functions of YOP and its successor YTS is to rejuvenate and foster the will to work.

There is one further set of arguments, associated with the worry about young people's attitudes. It is the view that much of the problem stems from a fundamental *misunderstanding* of some basic facts of economic life. This line is perhaps most clearly articulated by Sir Keith Joseph (1982) who in a written parliamentary answer said that, 'schools and business need to understand each other better ... schools and pupils need to be helped to understand how the nation earns its living in the world'. If pupils understood the process of wealth creation then it is thought that more would be attracted to careers in industry and commerce (particularly the more able), and would be better motivated to work.

Some commentators have interpreted all these trends in social class terms. Simply put, the analysis goes something like this. What we are witnessing is a straightforward working class revolt against an industrial market system that places them in uninteresting jobs with little scope for high earnings or self-improvement. In this analysis social and life skills courses are crude attempts at socializing potential manual workers into the system of industrial labour, whilst courses in 'how a nation earns its living' are no more than 'capitalist propaganda', masquerading as economics, for an ailing economic system.

The Pressure for Change

It is one thing to make a diagnosis of the problem, it is quite another to have that diagnosis accepted, and another still to persuade the schools to change.

We can identity three main areas of pressure on the schools. The first comes from central government; the second from the local employers and the local employment environment; the third pressure comes from ad hoc projects/movements specifically designed to change some elements of schooling. The DES and HM Inspectorate have issued a stream of reports all urging closer links between the 'real world' of employment (particularly industry and commerce) and the school curriculum. In terms of the broad thrust of political policy there is no significant difference between the political parties.

The second source of pressure is in some ways more powerful because it can be applied locally. Employers were noted for criticizing local schools in the middle seventies. It was they that delivered the broadside about deficiencies in 'basics' and social skills. More recently the sheer absence of employment for young people (and the reference point for this is nearly always the immediate locality, or at most the region) has at least raised the question with some schools — 'what are we teaching for?'

Our last source of pressure is a major source of change and a curiously British phenomenon. Because each school is more or less allowed to decide its own curriculum then curriculum change comes about by what often amounts to a sales campaign mounted by various agencies. The campaign can be about science teaching (the Nuffield campaigns), or about classics teaching (the Cambridge Classics Project) or health education (the various campaigns supported by the Health Education Council). Campaigns to get the school curriculum to draw closer to the industrial world and/or to produce more or better quality entrants to the world of employment have been particularly vigorous and numerous in the last decade. The unpublished Cooper Report commissioned by the DES to chart the schools-industry area, found fourteen major national projects working in the nation's schools and innumerable local endeavours. These national projects were spending £2.9m annually. Young Enterprise targeted itself on sixth-formers and tried to show them what was involved in running a company; Project Trident provided work experience for large numbers of school age youngsters; The Schools Council Careers and Guidance Project focussed on the process of vocational choice; a large number of projects focussed on the development of technology and engineering in the schools.

The School Reaction

How have schools reacted to all these pressures to change the process of schooling? The short answer is that overall there has not been a great deal of change. Schools in 1983 look remarkably similar to schools in 1973 despite all those sales campaigns and the virtual collapse of the job market for school leavers. This is not to deny that there have been changes, or even that the pace of change is quickening — both of these things are true — it is merely to assert that despite wholesale change in the economy there has been no wholesale change in the education system.

What changes there have been are interesting and warrant scrutiny, not least for their social class implications. Perhaps the dominant response from the schools is to concentrate even harder on the traditional subjects and the traditional examinations. If the competition for jobs is tougher then the pupils must become even more competitive. Teachers are well aware that one consequence of the job shortage is that employers have raised their entry qualifications for what jobs there are. And the link between academic qualifications and employment/unemployment which we show on table 1 is one which many teachers urge on their pupils.

If the major reaction has been 'the recipe as before — only better cooked', this is not to deny that there are other modes of adaptation that are of growing importance. One of these modes is for the school to spend more time on areas of study deemed to be more 'relevant' to the world of employment. This can take several forms. In the first place one has seen new 'subjects' come into the school curriculum, particularly in the technology area. Thus, the 'new' subject of craft, design and technology is gradually replacing the single subject craft specialisms (woodwork, metalwork etc.). Courses like modular technology are now appearing on the 'A' level syllabus. One factor holding some of these developments back is employer reaction. There is a great deal of evidence to suggest that employers take a very traditional view of qualifications — like most consumers they tend both to buy what they are familiar with and to accept the qualifications which the most able take. Dramatic evidence of this phenomenon was provided by the government 'think tank' report on education, training and industrial performance (Central Policy Review Staff, 1980). They showed that although employers preferred the more applied, industrially relevant subject content, when it came to expressing preference for named 'A' level subjects they opted for the traditional sciences like physics and chemistry. It is difficult to know how long it will be before these 'new' subjects become established — twenty years after the introduction of the CSE, many employers are still not clear what it signifies.

Not only are schools very gradually introducing a range of more 'relevant' 'O' and 'A' levels into the syllabus, but entirely new courses are also entering the school curriculum. One range of courses which can be described as vocational or pre-vocational are to be found in the sixth-form. Their existence owes as much to the entrepreneurial nature of examining boards like the RSA and City and Guilds, and the large increase in the numbers of pupils returning to the school in the sixth form (the new sixth) because there are no jobs, than it does to any explicit desire on the part of schools to feed the needs of industry.

Finally, there are a growing number of non-examinable courses in the fourth and fifth years of schooling that are set up to deal with a range of issues which it is generally agreed are 'important', but which either don't fit into traditional subjects, or it is felt do not merit a subject of their own. 'Industry' sits here along with health education, sex education, political education, and very often RE, careers and economics.

Many of these new courses have work experience as an integral part. Work experience, so it is argued, provides a good way of testing out relevant learning in a practical way, and of learning a range of things about the world of work that would be difficult to learn in schools. In fact the evidence for 'world of work' learning from work experience is scant (HMI, 1977; Jamieson, 1983). In general, it is most valued by schools for developing 'social and life skills', aiding the process of job choice and, by giving youngsters a trial run with an employer, promoting future employment prospects.

For many schools the heart of the interface between school and employment is the careers teacher(s). The careers teacher is most likely to be in charge of the work experience scheme. The dilemmas facing careers departments in schools are particularly acute in the present economic circumstances. The greatest problem is what to do and say about youth unemployment. Careers teachers seem horribly caught between putting even more effort into job acquisition skills (computer assisted vocational guidance; more practice at job applications, inter-viewing techniques, etc.), and facing the fact of unemployment head on. Many have sought a solution through greater concentration on social and life skills, having made the happy 'discovery' that skills demanded in adult *working* life are remarkably similar to those in adult life in general, irrespective of whether the adult is employed or not.

Teaching for Unemployment?

In general the teaching profession has strongly resisted the notion of teaching for unemployment. Most would agree with the sentiments expressed by John Tomlinson, then Chairman of the Schools Council,

> We utterly refute the notion that we should in the schools train children for unemployment. This is not what we are for, any more than we specifically train them for particular employment.[1]

The major response to unemployment as we have already observed is to concentrate even harder on the traditional curriculum to make the pupils more competitive in a tighter job market. Other responses are to draw more tightly towards the local employers, particularly, although not exclusively, through work experience. Courses which concentrate on leisure pursuits have increased in the schools but this has not been a major response. Preparing young people for self-employment is something which has been strongly supported by the Conservative government, and particularly the Department of Trade and Industry. A growing proportion of schools are doing work in the entrepreneurship area, largely by getting the pupils to form mini enterprises (Jamieson, 1984). The importance of this sector of the economy in job production, particularly for young people, however, is much exaggerated. (Bourne and Gould, 1983). Less common responses, and ones which schools find peculiarly difficult to handle, are teaching youngsters about welfare rights and how to survive in the informal economy (Watts, 1978).

The Technical and Vocational Education Initiative

It was against the background of little systematic reaction in the school system to the dramatic changes in the social and economic hinterland, that the government announced its Technical and Vocational Education Initiative (TVEI). The aim of the initiative (a pilot programme) is to introduce a variety of four-year courses of technical and vocational education for students between the ages of 14–18. Sixty LEAs are involved in a scheme costing £150m over five years.

There is a sense in which the scheme represents the government's loss of patience with the ability of the devolved education system to react to change. The government's determination to provide a large and radical initiative to change the balance of the curriculum can be seen by the way in which the change was instituted. There was no consultation with the usual professional interest groups. It has been argued that, 'the devisers of the TVEI were seemingly determined to act quickly and wanted to avoid having their radical ideas smothered in a consultative morass, or at least amended out of all recognition' (Moon and Richardson, 1984, p. 25).

Politically the TVEI is a significant educational initiative, not least because it is being run not by the DES, but by that dirigiste arm of government, the MSC. We might even look back on the initiative as the first stage of tighter state control of the curriculum. Yet if the TVEI is to alter the balance of the school curriculum it will have to resist being transmogrified by the education system. In particular, it will have to appeal to a broad spectrum of children (and their parents), and provide a set of qualifications that are widely accepted both by employers and further and higher education. These are formidable objectives even for the MSC.

The Social Class Implications of the Schools' Reactions

We have briefly charted the schools' reactions to the new economic scenario, but have only hinted at the social class implications of some of these adaptations. The most important point to make is that the school curriculum in this area, as in most areas, is differentiated according to the pupils' academic performance which is strongly class-based.

This point can be demonstrated by examining three features of the curriculum we have already discussed. First, work experience. Work experience is much more likely to be offered to the low achieving group and this group is strongly skewed towards the working class (Watts, 1983). The job placements tend to be at the lower end of the occupational hierarchy and there is clear evidence that working class pupils tend to end up in the working class jobs, whilst the few white collar jobs on offer are most likely to go to the sons and daughters of the middle class (Jamieson and Lightfoot, 1982). We might also add that work experience also tends to reinforce sex stereotyping (*Ibid*).

The social and life skills field is another area which is marked by differentiation according to social class. By and large social and life skills training is something which it is deemed is needed by the less able not the most able. As several commentators have pointed out, SLS teaching often seems predicated on a cultural deficit model, i.e. the working class pupils are in some sense deprived of the culture of the middle class (Atkinson, Rees, Shone and Williamson, 1982). The academically able middle class remain untouched by most of these developments. They continue to pursue the traditional academic routes through into higher education and what is left of the job market for young people.

Credentialling and Entry into Employment

In the current depressed economy in order for young people to get jobs it is ever more necessary for them to have some employment *credentials*. In general, it is surprising how well the traditional credentials, particularly 'O' and 'A' levels are holding up against the new competition. One reason for this is that employers do not, in general, distinguish between job *entry* requirements and job *performance* requirements. Indeed, as the London into Work Study (Townsend *et al*, 1982) showed many employers do not in fact know what is required to perform jobs in their work organizations. Employers simply ask for 'hard currency' qualifications that they believe will give them in the most general terms, 'the right sort of person'. There is no doubt that this entry system discriminates against the working class.

A rash of new qualifications have grown up to support the new curricula. Most of these come from the non-traditional examining bodies like the City and Guilds, BTEC and the RSA. Once again it is interesting to see the government giving a helping hand to 'market forces'. Under its initiative a consortium of these bodies have come forward to prepare a new qualification, the Certificate of Pre-Vocational Education (CPVE), which it is hoped might credential much of the TVEI and YTS. Will this be the new badge of the qualified industrial working class, replacing the CSE?

There are some important developments that may begin to alter this situation. The first of these is pupil profiling. Pupil profiling, particularly when it includes a wider range of qualities, experiences and activities than traditional school examinations — such things for example as the ability to perform practical tasks in a real work setting — might be of benefit to working class children simply because there is no reason to suppose that ability here would be skewed by social class. At the moment one has to counsel caution on pupil profiles, not least because what evidence we have indicates that very few schools have experience in producing them (Balogh, 1982), and that there are very considerable problems for schools in producing them (Goacher, 1983).

It is not clear whether the DES guidelines for pupil profiles, which are shortly to come into operation, will prevent profiling ending up as an assessment device for the low achievers. Pupil profiling is important in the debate about credentialling because it raises the possibility of the working class breaking through a major barrier to employment, a barrier which can hardly be justified in terms of the ability to do the job. Of far greater significance than pupil profiling, if only because it is highly likely that it will affect up to 70 per cent of school leavers, is the Youth Training Scheme. The existence of YTS could mean the virtual end of young people leaving school at 16 and moving straight into employment. Instead, the great majority of youngsters who leave at this age will now enter a one-year training scheme. For employers this will mean that in effect they have a whole year in which to assess the young person's suitability for employment. This should mean that sheer ability to perform the task — a quality never directly assessed before — will play a major role in entry to employment. Of course, one must realize that YTS is by no means a homogeneous scheme. It is clearly more advantageous for a young person to be on a Mode A scheme run by an employer, rather than a college-based Mode B. Even within Mode A there are some 'gilt edged' schemes run by major employers. Furthermore, entry to the different schemes is controlled, to an extent, by the Careers Service. There is every reason to expect that the Careers Service will unconsciously follow the well-worn social class pathways of selection, assisted by their knowledge of potential or actual examination results. YTS started in 1983 — it is much too soon to assess the result of this radical change in the educational landscape.

Conclusion

Education always seems to be at a 'turning point' — even at crisis point in these isles. And the 1980s don't appear to be an exception. What we need to remember in the context of the theme for these papers is that social class inequalities in relation to the education system have historically been particularly resistant to change. Two major developments, the expansion of higher education and the advent of comprehensive schools made surprisingly little difference.

What the current economic crisis, with its phenomenally high levels of youth unemployment, has done is to engender a close political scrutiny of the educational system. One of the distinguishing marks of the present government is its ability to challenge many of the established shibboleths in education, *and* to take radical action. The government's TVEI programme, has been born out of sheer frustration with the pace of change. All those projects and organizations trying to coax more technical and vocational work out of the schools just weren't making enough progress for the government. We believe that it is highly likely that a permanent shift will be made in Britain's schools towards a more industrially-oriented curriculum.

We have already suggested that YTS is potentially the most significant single development in the education system because it radically changes the destination of most school leavers. The significance of YTS will take time to work out. We suspect that much will depend on the youth unemployment figures *despite* the fact that YTS is part of a much wider vocational *training* initiative (NTI). One scenario could certainly be that economic recovery does occur and youth unemployment drops drastically. In such a situation we believe that many youngsters and employers would by-pass YTS, and life would continue much as before, both in schools and industry. In such a situation we could well see the emergence of a dual sector economy in this country much as one sees in many parts of the third world and Japan. Large firms and a much smaller public sector would recruit their top people through private schools and the universities. Their workers would come from 'gilt edged' YTS schemes. People working in this sector would be well paid and secure. In the other part of the economy a mass of smaller firms would recruit from the state schools. Work would be less congenial, less well paid and more insecure than in the corporate sector. In such circumstances we would truly be able to speak of 'two nations'.

Note

1   House of Commons Education, Science and Arts Committee (1981), para. 7.42.

References

ATKINSON, P., REES, T.L., SHONE, D. and WILLIAMSON, H., (1982) 'Social and life skills: The case of compensatory education', in REES, T.L. and ATKINSON, P. (Eds.)., *Youth Unemployment and State Intervention*, London, Routledge.

BALOGH, J. (1982), *Profile Reports for School Leavers*, York, Longman.

BANKS, M.H., MULLINGS, C., JACKSON, E.J., (1983) 'A bench mark for youth opportunities', *Employment Gazette*, 91, 3., March.

BOURNE, R. and GOULD, J. (1983) *Self-Sufficiency 16–25*, London, Kogan Page.

BOWLES, S. and GINTIS, H. (1976) *Schooling in Capitalist America*, London, Routledge and Kegan Paul.

CENTRAL POLICY REVIEW STAFF (1980) *Education Training and Industrial Performance*, London, HMSO.

DEPARTMENT OF EDUCATION AND SCIENCE (1983) *Statistical Bulletin 12/83*, Participation in education by the 16 to 19 age group and its association with the socio-economic characteristics of an area, London, HMSO.

GOACHER, B. (1983) *Recording Achievement at 16+*, York, Longman.

HER MAJESTY'S INSPECTORATE (1977), *Curriculum 11–16*, London, HMSO.

JAMIESON, I.M. (1983) 'Miracles or mirages: Some elements of pupil work experience', *British Journal of Guidance and Counselling*, 11, 2.

JAMIESON, I.M. (1984) 'Schools and enterprise', in WATTS, A.G. and MORAN, P. (Eds), *Education for Enterprise*, Cambridge, CRAC.

JAMIESON, I.M. and LIGHTFOOT, M. (1982) *Schools and Industry*, London, Methuen.

JOSEPH, SIR KEITH (1982), Written Parliamentary Answer, 29 July in DES Circular Letter SS5/19/01270, London, DES.

METCALFE, D. and RICHARDSON, R. (1982) 'Labour' in PREST, A.R. and COPPOCK, D.J. *The U.K. Economy*, London, Weidenfeld and Nicolson.

SMITH, A. (1981) 'The informal economy, *Lloyds Bank Review*, 141, July.

TOWNSEND, C. (1982) *London into Work Development Project*, Sussex, Institute of Manpower Studies, University of Sussex.

WATTS, A.G. (1978) 'The implications of school leaver unemployment for careers education in schools', *Journal of Curriculum Studies*, 10, 3.

WATTS, A.G. (Ed.) (1983) *Work Experience and Schools*, London, Heinemann.

Education and Social Class: Work: Discussion

Despite the development of comprehensive schools and the expansion of higher education, most children continue to face a system which favours the white middle-class male. Teachers' stereotyped attitudes, the emphasis on academic education, the teaching of facts rather than skills, the low status given to practical subjects, the external exam system geared to failing 80 per cent of pupils — these prevent all but the exceptional child to overcome a disadvantaged background and succeed. Our education system still ensures that the majority fail — and are seen to fail.

Both curriculum and teaching methods have changed little despite pressure from government, employers and independent research project groups. Nor have acute unemployment or cyclic depression forced a reshaping of what is taught and how. Schools are, in fact, becoming more selective and exam-oriented. Even the Youth Training Scheme is being developed with 'gilt-edged' schemes for a select few and college-based schemes for the rest.

The dilemma for teachers in comprehensive schools is to find ways to overcome the system's resistance to such changes and still ensure traditional academic success.

Five areas of schooling have to be changed in order to provide every child with the opportunities to learn and develop regardless of social class, gender or ethnic background. Such changes would offer the best preparation for adult life enabling people to go on learning through life and be capable of changing and adapting to new situations.

1   The development of whole school policies

Students would be far more ready to accept school if they were aware of and involved in the development and practice of whole school policies, such as strategies for learning.

2 Curriculum change

It is vital for all students to have a broad common core of experience which emphasizes the need to take responsibility for one's own life and which acknowledges a pupil's external influences and successes. This calls for a more flexible and imaginative use of school time, incorporating such schemes as day five, activity days and year-fortnights.

A common core of experience for pupils between 11 and 14 should include: organizing an activity themselves; working cooperatively in groups; exercising oral skills; developing critical skills such as using the media; a residential stay; work in the community; work shadowing — following someone on his or her job for a day; designing and making something; drama and music; testing oneself in some physical activity; presenting an extended piece of work; experience of some activity over an extended period of time; developing study skills; evaluation; using profiles to reflect on learning and to identify goals; opportunities for responsibility and involvement in school organization.

3 Changes in teaching

The main emphasis in teaching should be to produce confident, responsible and independent learners. Teachers should be aware of pupils' needs and respond to them sensitively, flexibly and creatively.

Examples of good practice for teachers include: providing opportunities for pupils to participate fully in lessons so that an atmosphere of trust is created; using simulations to construct as wide a variety of situations and experiences as possible which allow pupils to learn skills, concepts and to have opportunities for expressing their emotions; enriching lessons by bringing in fresh resources both from within the school and from the community; grouping pupils, such as working pairs of boy and girl, with carefully structured tasks to ensure that each initiates as well as cooperates; extending the use of music, drama, dance, art and writing; increasing the variety of sports options to lessen the influence of team games and their related culture.

4 Changes in pupil assessment and evaluation

The way all pupils in a school are assessed and evaluated should be changed to include the use of profiles and negotiated curricula validated by local community representatives but with national recognition and currency.

Profiles built up by pupils, parents and teachers can increase motivation by their recognition of a much wider range of qualities, experiences and activities which help pupils to value and promote themselves.

One recommended scheme for assessment and evaluation is the Royal Society of Arts Education for Capability Scheme. Here pupils have a choice about what they learn by using negotiated courses; peer pressure is reduced through greater self-determination; the integral evaluation in the scheme keeps pupils aware of their goals; there are opportunities for both individual and group involvement as well as time for extended work; the absence of an externally imposed exam enables those who have failed under the traditional exam system to have a real chance to prove themselves and the more able pupils to extend themselves further; validation by the community allows governors, local employers and others to share in what young people learn.

5 *Greater involvement in school by parents and the community*

Pupils are more likely to be influenced by parents and other adults who take an active part in the life of the school. Evidence from successful community schools shows more regular attendance by fourth and fifth-year pupils and improved exam results.

Gender and Social Class

Rosemary Deem

The first important comment that needs to be made about gender and social class is that gender is not merely a dimension of social class. Secondly, gender and class cannot simply be lumped together or accumulated to form a total set of disadvantages or advantages for a given social group. Thirdly, we cannot assume, as many do, that class issues and the eradication of class-based inequalities in education should necessarily take precedence over gender issues and gender-based inequalities in terms of education policies and political priorities.

But to say that there is no simple connection between gender and class is not the same as saying that there are *no* connections between the two. Both are important social divisions, both are reflected in educational practices and processes, both are social constructs, both are found in capitalist societies. But whereas it is possible for individuals to change their social class through upward or downward mobility, it is not possible for most people to change their gender; the latter is a social construction with biological roots (however unimportant these are or have become) the former has no natural or physiological basis.

It has often been said, particularly by feminists, that gender divisions and their transmission through education have been ignored in educational debates, whereas class has been a central concern of those debates, particularly in the period since 1944. It is not, however, the case that gender divisions have been ignored; many official reports and documents have alluded to them, but have not seen them as problematic (Deem, 1981; Wolpe, 1974). What is relatively recent is the view that educational gender differentiation and gender discrimination is as unfair to human potential and social justice as class differentiation and discrimination in schooling. Because of this belated recognition of the political and social importance of gender divisions, it can be argued that the pursuit of class equality through education has actually obscured as well as hindered the pursuit of gender equality within the educational system, since the strategies advanced to help eradicate class divisions are not necessarily those which contribute to the eradication of gender divisions. For example the shift towards comprehensive schools during the 1960s and 1970s was accompanied by a parallel move towards coeducation; but the latter was never publicly debated nor its effects on gender discrimination fully considered (Weinberg, 1979 and 1981; Deem, 1984).

Gender and Class — the Interconnections

There are a number of ways in which these interconnections may be seen. Barrett (1980) categorizes them in this way:

1 That gender is absorbed completely by class, such that it is class which forms the major determinants of an individual's major experiences and life chances. Most conventional social science theory on class takes this assumption for granted, and allocates all but single adult women living alone, to a class position on the basis of their father's or husband's occupation.

2 That gender and class are independent systems of oppression with no connections, except that empirically both are found in capitalist societies. This argument takes several forms, but almost all make use of the concept of patriarchy (briefly, male dominance over women). One form is to argue that women constitute a social class in their own right (Morgan, 1975).

3 That class divisions are exacerbated by gender discrimination and segregation in the labour market (Westergaard and Resler, 1976); that is class and gender are cumulative in their effects on inequality. But the class position taken into account here is *male* class position, whereas gender becomes a shorthand for *women*. Yet, says Barrett, if we look at attempts to compare the occupations of married women with those of their husbands we find that such comparisons place many women in a different social class category from their husband (Garnsey, 1978; Brown 1978), which just points out the inadequacy of the categories class and gender being used in attempts like that of Westergaard and Resler.

4 That there are links between gender and class, and that it is

possible to partially reconcile the two, viewing class and relations of production under capitalism as important, whilst still perceiving differences between the relationship of women to the class structure and the relationship of men to that class structure. For women this link to the class structure of capitalist societies involves a dual relationship, argues Barrett (1980), with education playing a central role in this relationship:

> The education and training that a woman receives by virtue of her class background provide a highly significant contribution to the position she will occupy in the labour force. Yet the relationship she has to the class structure by virtue of her wage labour (or her ownership of the means of production) will be substantially influenced by the mediation of this direct relationship through dependence on men and responsibility for domestic labour and childcare. For working class women this may result in simultaneous direct exploitation by capital via their own wage labour and indirect exploitation via . . . a male breadwinner. For bourgeois women this may result in simultaneous ownership of, yet lack of control over, capital. (p. 139)

This last position brings us closer to finding a relationship between gender and social class which is both explanatory, and helpful, in examining what has happened to these two social divisions within the educational system. Further, Willis (1977) has pointed to the centrality of definitions of masculinity to the culture of younger working class males, and to the ways in which entry to paid employment is conceptualized as being crucially important to notions of appropriate working class male behaviour and interests; whereas McRobbie and McCabe (1981) have noted that for young working class females, notions of femininity whilst not ignoring paid work, focus much more on relationships with men, and fantasies about future marriage and motherhood. So gender and class do seem to be linked, but the connections between the two are such as to hold in question the assumption that what is educationally good for working class boys, is also necessarily good for working class girls.

Educational Inequality and the Shift to Mixed Secondary Schools

There have been some considerable controversies recently over the extent to which comprehensive schools have aided or reduced working class attainment (Berliner, 1983; Marks and Cox, 1983). This chapter is not the appropriate place to develop those debates, but what it is important to do is to consider seriously whether mixed comprehensive schools have actually contributed significantly to greater educational equality for girls, whether of middle or working class origins, or whether the search for class equality in education has hindered sex equality. The recent mixed versus single sex schools debate has largely been revived by feminists (Deem, 1984; Spender, 1982) and outside of the early decades of this century (Brehony, 1984) there has been little actual discussion of the issue; it has been *assumed* that coeducation must be better socially and academically, for both sexes. Some doubt began to be cast on this belief in 1975, when a DES survey on curricular differences between boys and girls in secondary schools found that girls were more likely to choose science subjects in single sex schools than in mixed schools, even though single sex schools were less likely to have good science facilities. Nevertheless, the survey warned against using its data to support an argument for single sex schools as opposed to mixed ones. Later studies have shown that it is statistically extremely difficult to untangle class, gender and attainment differences, in order to discover whether single sex schools have actually contributed to gender equality in education. An ILEA research report in 1982 on sex differences and achievement, based on data from the period when ILEA still had many single sex schools, found that 15–16 year olds (boys and girls) in ILEA schools in 1980 did achieve higher grades and a broader range of subjects in GCE 'O' levels and CSEs than did pupils in mixed schools. But the report also noted that these findings could partly be accounted for by the differences in ability range at entry to the schools surveyed in 1975 (ILEA didn't abolish 11+ selection until 1977). With this difference taken into account it was found that 'There was no significant difference in examination achievement for either sex between single sex and mixed schools' (ILEA, 1982, p. 10). An extensive analysis of available evidence on mixed and single sex schools carried out by Ann Bone for the Equal Opportunities Commission (1983) confirms the ILEA survey findings. Although girls in single sex schools do appear to do much better than those in mixed schools in all academic subjects, when ability is taken into account this difference virtually disappears, although there are still small advantages apparent for girls' performances in maths and physics in single-sex schools (Stevens, 1983).

But if the shift to coeducational schools has not particularly hindered girls' academic attainment it has certainly not improved it. As the Bone study (1983) and other researchers have noted, girls are failing to achieve the same education as boys regardless of type of school. And for those girls who would formerly have gone to a single sex grammar school, their chances of academic success at a mixed comprehensive appear to be reduced. The shift to mixed schools has also had another serious effect for women, one which is never taken into account when people assess the impact and achievements of comprehensive schools in terms of social class equality. The proportion of secondary headships filled by women has dropped by nearly 10 per cent since 1963, according to a survey of eighty-six LEAs by the Women's National Commission (Wilce, 1983), and this decline is largely attributed to the virtual disappearance of single-sex secondary schools from most LEAs. Women are much less likely to be appointed as heads of mixed schools, whilst it is not uncommon for men to be appointed heads of all-girl schools. The declining number of women heads is not just serious because of its effects on the promotion chances of women teachers, but also because it means that girls in mixed secondary schools are much less likely to see women in positions of authority, and hence the argument that women are subordinate to men in public spheres of life becomes strengthened. Yet the belief that mixed schools are important to the achievement of equal opportunities persists. When Labour took control of the ILEA in 1981, one of their concerns was to get rid of remaining single sex schools, and the Labour majority group on Liverpool City Council's 1983 plans for comprehensive reorganization of that City's schools had as a central plank the cessation of single sex schools. What is good for class equality — a social and ability mix — must also be good for gender goes the argument, although often it is not even as explicit as that, or even as thought through. Because the critiques of tripartism in the 1950s and 1960s were all about class inequalities, gender inequalities received scant attention until very recently from educationists, and some of the changes made with the genuine intention of reducing class inequality may well have increased gender inequality. Shaw (1984) argues that the formal selection processes of the 11+ examination and the tripartite system have been replaced by informal modes of selection, based on a combination of class and gender. This operates through social processes, many of the interpersonal kind, which flourish in the mixed settings of coeducational schools.

The difficulty is that support for single sex schools from parents often reveals a social class bias, with such education being readily available in the private sector and with most remaining single sex schools in the state sector being grammar schools. Hence those concerned with achieving social equality in education have tended to be even more convinced that single-sex schools are a bad thing in themselves, without pausing to think that social inequality has more than one dimension.

Girls and Attainment in Comprehensive Schools

If we move from the mixed/single sex schools argument itself, towards a consideration of how girls have actually performed academically in comprehensives, then we find that there are at least two strands to the arguments. One is whether boys, of all social class origins, receive a superior education compared with that received by girls (Wolpe, 1982) and the second is the range of subjects in which girls or boys attempt and pass GCE and CSE examinations. If we take the first-mentioned strand, it is evident that class differences must play their part in determining who receives a superior education. There are strong historical grounds for arguing that working class pupils have generally, since the nineteenth century received an education inferior to that received by middle and upper class pupils. Educational provision this century has been strongly marked by class differentiation, something which persists even in comprehensive secondary education, especially with the virtual disappearance of bussing to achieve social and ethnic mixing. Of course not all working class boys are coming out of school with large numbers of 'O' level or higher grade CSE passes, in a wide range of subjects from French to physics and maths, any more than are all working class girls leaving school with no formal qualifications, never having studied the physical sciences or taken an exam in maths or technical drawing. Nevertheless, within class groupings, the available evidence does suggest that gender differences do have considerable effect upon the *experiences* of schooling. For instance one of the most widespread findings of research on gender and schools is that boys are much more noisy, take more teacher time, speak more frequently and are often more disruptive in classrooms than are girls (Spender, 1982;

Clarricoates, 1980). Girls, of course, find their own 'spaces' in schools and develop their own sub-cultures, but the evidence suggests that they are generally less visible, less noisy and talk less to teachers, and are talked to less by teachers, than boys (McCabe, 1981; Willis, 1977). The social experiences of education are thus not likely to be the same for working class boys as they are for working class girls. Mixed classrooms do tend to transmit messages to girls about male-female power relations, the confidence and assertivenesses of men, and the subordinate place of women, irrespective of the levels of academic attainment achieved by either sex. In this sense, whilst many other indications may suggest that the education of working class boys is inferior to that of middle class boys, such education is generally a superior social experience to that received by working class girls, even though perhaps both genders receive an education which could be greatly improved. Nothing in the history of mixed comprehensive schools so far suggests that if we start to solve problems about class inequalities, gender inequalities are automatically reduced at the same time (Stantonbury Campus Sexism in Education Group, 1984). It may be more 'natural' (whatever that implies) to have both genders in one school, it may replicate the 'real world'. But the 'real world' in which we live has strong and inequitable gender divisions just as much as it has strong inequitable class divisions, and to replicate that real world in mixed schools may mean replicating precisely those inequitable relationships and attitudes which characterize male dominance over women within class cultures as well as across and between them.

If we turn now to the second strand of the argument, that about the relative academic achievements of girls and boys, we come up against problems in relation to the categories used to assess and collate statistical information. These categories are often either gender-blind or class-blind, or more usually both. Thus the DES statistics on school leavers categorize by gender but not by class. The National Child Development Study (a longitudinal analysis of all people born in England, Scotland or Wales during 3–9 March 1958) whilst categorizing much of its evidence by class, has not organized all its evidence in terms of gender categories and its use of class categories leaves much to be desired, since it is based primarily on fathers' occupation (Education Digest, 1983). However, DES statistics and the National Child Development Study do show us that overall there are two areas of significant difference between boys and girls of all social classes. One is that the NCDS found

Marked sex differences ... in the career and educational plans of these young people ... Boys were most likely to be hoping for a job in the engineering industry, whereas many girls foresaw clerical jobs. The two sexes were equally likely to plan to stay at school beyond 16 but boys were more likely to intend to go on to a university or polytechnic, or to take a job which entailed part time study. Girls were relatively more likely to plan to go to a college of education or some other form of higher education, or to leave at 16 for a job with no part-time study'. (Education Digest of NCDS, 1983, p. iii)

The other significant difference is that if we look at GCE 'O' level and CSE attempts, and passes, although girls overall get more passes than boys, the subjects in which girls pass (or which they attempt) are not the same as those which boys pass or attempt. Now it may be argued that this differentiation is based largely on free option 'choices' by pupils. Indeed HMI in the 1979 Secondary Schools Survey suggested that for fourth and fifth-year pupils in the 384 schools surveyed, only English, games, RE and careers education were usually 'core' subjects, and a more recent study of inner and outer London borough secondary school prospectives also confirms this (Weeks, 1983). The problem is that pupil choice is always hinged about with constraints (Ling, 1983), in particular constraints of class and gender, and the 'choices' made are a product of socialization experiences into deeply-rooted social divisions within the family, peer group and community as well as in school, predicated on the gender divisions found in the structure of society as a whole. Girls and boys may 'choose' which subjects they take but it is not a free choice, and the social conditions under which those choices are made are such that pupils have little or no control over them. The pilot (increasingly less pilot-like as the number of schemes expands) Technical and Vocational Education Initiative schemes for 14–18 year olds in schools and FE colleges, financed by the Manpower Services Commission, currently being developed by LEAs, may well, despite the existence of a criterion which specifies that provision must be made for both sexes, increase the extent of curriculum differentiation along gender lines for the age-groups included within its remit, since the labour market to which TVEI is directed, is heavily sex-segregated as well as class-divided. What the available evidence from DES statistics shows is that in GCE 'O' and 'A' levels, and CSEs, girls and boys are actually achieving passes in a gender-segregated range of subjects. So, regardless of their social class origin, the sexes are not leaving school on an equal footing. Girls whose exam passes tend to include the humanities, domestic science, commercial subjects, biology and social studies, cannot compete on level terms with boys within any social class grouping for jobs, and for further and higher education. The shift of emphasis towards science and technology in employment prospects and the balance between subjects in higher education means that those without qualifications in science, mathematical and technological subjects, are disadvantaged whatever they decide to do after leaving school. Whilst obviously many of the disadvantaged are working class leavers, some of whom have no formal qualifications at all, or only low-grade CSEs, girls are disadvantaged even when they have formal qualifications, because those qualifications are in a different range of subjects from those possessed by boys and required increasingly by employers and higher education entry. Unless we can move away from option choices, in whatever form they occur, for pupils in the later years of secondary schooling, curriculum differentiation by gender is likely to persist, even if we were able to ensure greater social class equality in the distribution of examination passes.

Why Gender is as Important as Class in Educational Reform

Shaw (1984) has argued that one of the reasons why educational reformers of the left have paid more attention to class than to gender is because class is seen as a political issue for men and women; gender inequalities are seen as a political issue for women only, and hence lack the political 'pull' and importance of class. But as Arnot (1984) has pointed out, gender inequalities involve men as much as women, and we cannot really solve the issue of women's inequality in education without tackling the issue of men's education too. In our society, a gender and a class position are both inescapable; but, of course, there is no gender equivalent of upward social mobility! Clearly it is necessary to restate the importance of both class and gender to political agendas, especially in the field of education. Male dominance over women may be in part attributable to capitalism, but it existed prior to the development of capitalism, has its own logic and determinants, and cannot be relied upon to disappear with a change of economic system and norms of resource distribution. Whilst those who seek change in education continue to see class and class inequalities as the major evil, gender inequalities will continue to be ignored or even increased by the

Table 1: C.S.E. AND G.C.E. EXAMINATIONS C.S.E. All modes results, 1971 and 1974 to 1981 Pupils achieving Grade 5 or better

	1971	1974[1]	1975	1976	1977	1978	1979	1980	1981	Percentage increase 1976–1978
English[2]										
Boys	97,872	177,466	176,930	194,097	238,946	251,800	265,432	277,559	273,111	40.7
Girls	86,416	183,027	182,435	201,392	241,754	254,755	270,991	285,038	281,479	39.8
Total	184,288	360,493	359,365	395,489	480,700	506,555	536,423	562,597	554,590	40.2
History[2]										
Boys	34,668	55,655	55,727	59,227	66,190	70,952	70,812	72,529	75,827	28.0
Girls	33,326	56,887	57,130	61,497	69,789	75,935	77,054	78,718	82,305	33.8
Total	69,994	112,542	112,857	120,724	135,979	146,887	147,866	151,247	158,132	31.6
French[2]										
Boys	23,392	35,713	35,934	39,334	42,242	45,076	47,261	49,435	52,703	34.6
Girls	33,444	57,452	57,813	63,459	73,041	78,395	84,392	90,360	95,131	49.9
Total	56,836	93,165	93,747	102,793	115,283	123,471	131,653	139,795	147,834	43.8
Art and craft[2]										
Boys	30,795	58,780	58,289	62,436	69,446	69,394	74,315	81,100	80,211	28.5
Girls	27,011	54,986	54,721	59,284	71,740	66,157	71,271	78,238	78,871	33.0
Total	57,806	113,766	113,010	121,720	141,186	135,551	145,586	159,338	159,082	30.7
Other arts subjects										
Boys	16,357	25,996	25,612	28,595	39,083	43,355	44,867	46,407	48,583	69.9
Girls	26,923	46,335	45,820	50,427	61,803	70,305	71,133	75,048	77,954	54.6
Total	43,280	72,331	71,432	79,022	100,886	113,660	116,000	121,455	126,537	60.1
Mathematics[2,3]										
Boys	90,058	144,786	144,176	155,106	183,466	194,904	204,530	214,852	225,095	45.1
Girls	78,134	135,508	134,895	147,461	179,031	197,332	211,781	229,449	239,429	62.4
Total	168,192	280,294	279,071	302,567	362,497	392,236	416,311	444,301	464,524	53.5
Physics[2]										
Boys	48,439	72,818	72,498	75,425	84,253	82,553	98,525	103,714	110,011	45.9
Girls	4,888	9,672	9,593	10,130	12,085	13,696	18,809	21,383	24,615	143.0
Total	53,327	82,490	82,091	85,555	96,338	96,249	117,334	125,097	134,626	57.4
Biology[2]										
Boys	16,551	33,628	33,258	36,640	46,286	50,609	52,434	53,533	57,673	57.4
Girls	38,740	74,857	74,714	77,547	97,688	106,433	117,489	123,608	132,380	70.7
Total	55,291	108,485	107,972	114,187	143,974	157,042	169,923	177,141	190,053	66.4
Technical drawing[2]										
Boys	48,049	66,950	66,400	60,297	70,409	73,461	82,793	84,180	85,589	41.9
Girls	450	852	838	889	1,538	2,126	2,793	3,157	3,563	300.8
Total	48,499	67,802	67,238	61,186	71,947	75,587	85,586	87,337	89,152	45.7

									%
Metalwork and woodwork[2]									
Boys	53,403	86,751	86,126	94,130	107,784	106,575	110,423	111,763	113,996	21.1
Girls	168	520	511	701	1,039	1,695	1,725	1,830	2,027	189.2
Total	53,571	87,271	86,637	94,831	108,823	108,270	112,148	113,593	116,023	22.3
Other science or technical subjects									
Boys	51,383	101,526	100,815	115,042	134,257	152,773	155,383	161,940	166,537	44.8
Girls	16,799	37,019	36,774	41,848	50,667	61,687	69,042	76,053	81,851	95.6
Total	68,182	138,545	137,589	156,890	184,924	214,460	224,425	237,993	248,388	58.3
Geography[2]									
Boys	50,309	76,399	76,373	82,329	90,961	95,268	99,395	99,779	107,294	30.3
Girls	34,816	56,432	56,520	61,361	66,730	69,214	73,102	73,492	78,941	28.7
Total	85,125	132,831	132,893	143,690	157,691	164,482	172,497	173,271	186,235	29.6
Domestic subjects[2,4]									
Boys	1,526	5,353	5,287	7,253	9,277	9,722	11,500	10,658	11,189	54.3
Girls	57,449	105,154	104,606	114,508	129,372	128,702	145,720	148,530	153,456	34.0
Total	58,975	110,507	109,893	121,761	138,649	138,424	157,220	159,188	164,645	35.2
Commercial subjects[2]									
Boys	5,821	9,634	9,453	10,749	13,435	14,265	15,002	15,272	16,523	53.7
Girls	27,398	47,433	46,746	49,710	58,413	64,440	68,859	69,259	69,681	40.2
Total	33,219	57,067	56,199	60,459	71,848	78,705	83,861	84,531	86,204	42.6
Other social science or vocational subjects[5]									
Boys	11,148	34,898	34,649	39,094	55,928	56,337	56,694	58,430	61,504	57.3
Girls	10,844	37,935	37,488	43,487	65,410	67,265	68,275	71,352	74,856	72.1
Total	21,992	72,833	72,137	82,581	121,338	123,602	124,969	129,782	136,360	65.1
All subjects[2,6]									
Boys	581,771	986,353	981,527	1,059,754	1,251,963	1,317,044	1,389,366	1,441,151	1,485,846	40.2
Girls	476,806	904,069	900,604	983,701	1,180,100	1,258,137	1,352,436	1,425,515	1,476,539	50.1
Total	1,058,577	1,890,422	1,882,131	2,043,455	2,432,063	2,575,181	2,741,802	2,866,666	2,962,385	45.0
of which									
Mode 1	875,144	1,442,230	1,434,750	1,540,734	1,743,550	1,828,628	1,965,048	2,071,187	2,169,884	40.8
Mode 2	30,497	44,374	46,690	47,104	62,166	73,553	71,424	72,435	71,548	51.9
Mode 3	152,936	403,818	400,691	455,617	626,347	673,000	705,330	723,044	720,953	58.2
Total arts	412,204	752,297	750,411	819,748	974,034	1,026,124	1,077,528	1,134,432	1,146,175	39.8
Total science and technology	447,062	764,887	760,598	815,216	968,503	1,043,844	1,125,727	1,185,462	1,242,766	52.4
Total social science/vocational	199,811	373,238	371,122	408,491	489,526	505,213	538,547	546,772	573,444	41.4

The exceptional increase in the number of candidates in 1974 follows the raising of the school leaving age to 16 the previous year.

1 Including results achieved by candidates sitting examinations held in connection with the joint CSE/GCE 16+ feasibility, and development studies, separate details of which are given in table 25.
2 Including arithmetic.
3 Including cookery and needlework.
4 Including English economic history, economic and social studies
5 Excluding shorthand, typewriting and related subjects.
Source: HMSO (1983) *DES Statistics of School Leavers 1981*, London, HMSO.

Table 2: CSE AND GCE EXAMINATIONS Results at GCE Ordinary level, 1971 and 1974 to 1981 Summar examination

	1971	1974	1975[1]	1976[1]	1977[1]	1978[1]	1979[1]	1980[1]	1981[1]	Percentage increase 1976-1981
					Passes					
English language[2]										
Boys	88,226	102,598	106,958	109,609	113,098	114,155	116,728	114,477	115,363	5.2
Girls	108,058	130,258	145,564	146,376	150,169	154,409	157,622	154,015	158,176	8.1
Total	196,284	232,856	252,522	255,985	263,267	268,564	274,350	268,492	273,539	6.9
English literature[2]										
Boys	48,067	52,586	53,408	53,571	57,118	58,573	58,414	56,271	62,338	16.4
Girls	76,895	81,368	83,252	83,669	88,234	91,482	93,462	95,209	97,665	16.7
Total	124,962	133,954	136,660	137,240	145,352	150,055	151,876	151,480	160,003	16.6
History[2]										
Boys	33,138	35,990	39,476	39,725	38,830	38,692	39,066	35,672	35,848	-9.8
Girls	36,560	38,528	38,118	40,161	38,090	38,627	39,486	40,704	40,630	1.2
Total	69,698	74,518	77,594	79,886	76,920	77,319	78,552	76,376	76,478	-4.3
Latin[2]										
Boys	12,837	9,553	9,828	10,412	11,000	10,470	10,288	9,767	9,249	-11.2
Girls	14,193	11,008	10,930	12,665	11,814	11,014	10,849	10,653	10,129	-20.0
Total	27,030	20,561	20,758	23,077	22,814	21,484	21,137	20,420	19,378	-16.0
French[2]										
Boys	35,087	35,364	37,003	36,506	37,806	38,360	38,297	40,161	39,014	6.9
Girls	47,214	50,328	51,556	50,955	52,864	54,957	56,929	59,124	59,564	16.9
Total	82,301	85,692	88,559	87,461	90,670	93,317	95,226	99,285	98,578	12.7
German										
Boys	8,452	9,762	10,024	10,115	10,649	11,974	11,668	11,760	11,868	17.3
Girls	12,152	14,167	14,403	14,750	15,504	16,038	17,896	19,150	19,599	32.9
Total	20,604	23,929	24,427	24,865	26,153	28,012	29,564	30,910	31,467	26.6
Art[2]										
Boys	22,991	25,965	27,498	29,645	29,817	28,511	29,154	30,357	31,924	7.7
Girls	33,051	37,207	38,200	39,889	39,999	40,621	41,356	43,699	48,092	20.6
Total	56,042	63,172	65,698	69,534	69,816	69,132	70,510	74,056	80,016	15.1
Other art subjects[2]										
Boys	21,200	24,049	22,953	25,790	27,529	27,685	27,382	31,923	30,702	19.0
Girls	40,442	42,626	44,452	45,505	47,090	47,725	50,454	53,360	56,215	23.5
Total	61,642	66,675	67,405	71,295	74,619	75,410	77,836	85,283	86,917	21.9
Mathematics[2,3]										
Boys	99,377	103,878	107,825	115,312	123,279	129,339	134,479	138,577	142,919	23.9
Girls	53,407	59,234	61,211	66,712	71,312	76,918	83,366	89,083	95,484	43.1
Total	152,784	163,112	169,036	182,024	194,591	206,257	217,845	227,660	238,403	31.0

										%
Physics²										
Boys	48,390	53,621	58,859	61,142	65,277	68,592	73,635	76,156	77,396	26.6
Girls	13,019	14,736	16,120	16,587	19,061	20,738	23,958	26,016	27,338	64.8
Total	61,409	68,357	74,979	77,729	84,338	89,330	97,593	102,172	104,734	34.7
Chemistry²										
Boys	35,441	40,654	43,237	44,560	46,805	48,768	52,314	54,452	54,945	23.3
Girls	14,747	18,490	20,086	20,782	22,235	25,756	29,113	28,118	33,045	59.0
Total	50,188	59,144	63,323	65,342	69,040	74,524	81,427	82,570	87,990	34.7
Biology²										
Boys	31,760	38,874	42,991	44,963	46,488	48,267	48,524	50,077	50,570	12.5
Girls	55,663	60,979	67,518	66,361	68,756	71,905	72,097	75,082	78,138	17.7
Total	87,423	99,853	110,509	111,324	115,244	120,172	120,621	125,159	128,708	15.6
Other science or technical subjects²										
Boys	63,531	59,440	62,502	64,600	67,358	69,299	72,244	74,961	76,544	18.5
Girls	9,578	10,625	9,661	10,616	11,294	10,754	10,783	11,371	10,815	1.9
Total	73,109	70,065	72,163	75,216	78,652	80,053	83,027	86,332	87,359	16.1
Economics⁴										
Boys	22,091	25,732	27,963	27,113	29,724	29,716	30,376	30,141	29,307	8.1
Girls	15,285	19,516	21,382	21,209	25,025	26,745	27,802	28,399	28,528	34.5
Total	37,376	45,248	49,345	48,322	54,749	56,461	58,178	58,540	57,835	19.7
Geography²										
Boys	48,770	54,703	55,735	54,602	58,937	60,152	61,692	63,081	64,594	18.3
Girls	41,249	45,558	43,346	43,572	43,485	44,180	46,302	46,947	48,912	12.3
Total	90,019	100,261	99,081	98,174	102,422	104,332	107,994	110,028	113,506	15.6
Other social science or vocational subjects²										
Boys	23,048	23,177	25,182	26,036	26,278	29,735	29,764	31,197	33,203	27.5
Girls	58,782	69,866	70,190	79,517	83,587	85,825	89,880	94,850	96,863	21.8
Total	81,830	93,043	95,372	105,553	109,865	115,560	119,644	126,047	130,066	23.2
All subjects										
Boys	642,406	695,946	731,442	753,701	789,993	812,288	834,025	849,030	865,784	14.9
Girls	630,295	704,494	735,989	759,326	788,519	817,694	851,355	875,780	919,193	19.7
Total	1,272,701	1,400,440	1,467,431	1,513,027	1,578,512	1,629,982	1,685,380	1,724,810	1,774,977	17.3
Total arts	638,563	701,357	733,623	749,343	769,611	783,293	799,051	806,302	826,376	10.3
Total science and technology	424,913	460,531	490,010	511,635	541,865	570,336	600,513	623,893	647,194	26.5
Total social science/vocational	209,225	238,552	243,798	252,049	267,036	276,353	285,816	294,615	301,407	19.6

1 Passes cover grades A-C awarded.
2 Including results achieved by candidates sitting examinations held in connection with the joint CSE/GCE 16+ feasibility and development studies.
3 Including additional commercial and statistical mathematics.
4 Including English economic history and British constitution.
Source: HMSO (1983) *DES Statistics of School Leavers 1981*, London, HMSO.

Table 3: C.S.E. AND G.C.E. EXAMINATIONS Passes at G.C.E. Advanced level, 1971 and 1974 to 1981 Summer examination

	1971	1974	1975	1976	1977	1978	1979	1980	1981	Percentage Increase 1976–1981
English literature										
Boys	14,574	14,564	14,352	14,950	14,614	13,901	13,318	13,572	13,461	−10.0
Girls	26,348	27,924	28,729	29,785	29,831	30,145	29,736	30,665	31,258	4.9
Total	40,922	42,488	43,081	44,735	44,445	44,046	43,054	44,237	44,719	0.0
History[3]										
Boys	12,686	12,420	12,440	12,440	13,436	12,415	11,945	12,112	11,993	−5.8
Girls	11,974	12,048	12,043	12,093	13,130	12,834	12,328	12,829	13,058	3.0
Total	24,660	24,468	24,533	24,523	26,566	25,249	24,273	24,941	25,051	−1.4
Latin[3]										
Boys	1,852	1,348	1,231	1,119	1,142	1,098	1,095	1,000	1,045	−6.6
Girls	2,051	1,566	1,447	1,277	1,207	1,382	1,244	1,204	1,300	1.8
Total	3,903	2,914	2,678	2,396	2,449	2,480	2,339	2,204	2,345	−2.1
French										
Boys	6,022	5,356	5,277	5,391	5,576	6,539	6,854	5,107	5,131	−4.8
Girls	11,426	11,124	10,974	11,262	11,886	11,980	12,259	12,617	12,911	14.6
Total	17,448	16,480	16,251	16,653	17,462	18,519	19,113	17,724	18,042	8.3
German										
Boys	2,151	2,098	2,044	2,035	2,095	1,993	2,174	2,128	2,134	4.9
Girls	3,428	3,443	3,977	3,668	4,004	4,009	4,325	4,419	4,772	30.1
Total	5,579	5,541	6,021	5,703	6,099	6,002	6,499	6,547	6,906	21.1
Art										
Boys	5,562	6,133	6,346	6,805	7,466	6,730	6,634	6,354	6,768	−0.5
Girls	8,086	9,053	9,608	9,941	10,522	9,926	8,859	10,330	11,063	11.3
Total	13,648	15,186	15,954	16,746	17,988	16,656	15,493	16,684	17,831	6.5
Other arts subjects[3]										
Boys	4,662	4,780	4,836	5,103	5,491	5,245	5,204	5,163	5,381	5.4
Girls	7,071	7,346	7,895	7,875	8,465	8,626	8,300	8,852	9,884	25.5
Total	11,733	12,176	12,731	12,978	13,956	13,871	13,504	14,015	15,265	17.6
Mathematics[2]										
Boys	34,472	33,646	34,663	38,317	37,393	39,803	42,507	42,563	45,852	19.7
Girls	9,014	9,531	10,011	10,235	10,876	11,849	13,433	14,827	16,467	60.9
Total	43,486	43,177	44,674	48,552	48,269	51,652	55,440	57,390	62,319	28.4
Physics										
Boys	22,224	22,591	22,980	23,038	25,158	26,515	27,753	28,778	29,598	28.5
Girls	4,684	5,059	5,082	4,855	5,478	5,837	6,465	6,856	7,396	52.3
Total	26,908	27,650	28,062	27,873	30,636	32,352	34,218	35,634	36,994	32.6

Chemistry									
Boys	15,791	16,062	16,141	16,465	18,922	19,708	20,792	20,714	21,771	32.2
Girls	5,346	6,632	6,614	7,008	7,914	8,371	9,294	10,083	10,821	54.4
Total	21,137	22,694	22,755	23,473	26,836	28,079	30,086	30,797	32,592	38.8
Biology, botany and zoology									
Boys	8,547	11,010	10,980	11,723	12,678	13,145	12,485	12,531	12,628	7.7
Girls	8,683	10,647	10,888	10,902	12,801	14,154	14,485	15,707	16,410	50.5
Total	17,230	21,657	21,868	22,625	25,479	27,299	26,970	28,238	29,038	28.3
Other science or technical subjects									
Boys	6,611	6,215	5,480	6,429	7,003	6,633	5,991	5,901	5,977	−7.0
Girls	574	647	946	1,151	1,051	1,142	1,092	1,029	845	−26.6
Total	7,185	6,862	6,426	7,580	8,054	7,775	7,083	6,930	6,822	−10.0
Economics²									
Boys	19,800	19,933	21,786	24,116	24,657	24,173	24,245	22,937	22,897	−5.1
Girls	6,111	7,236	8,404	9,783	10,402	11,670	12,607	11,939	13,453	37.5
Total	25,911	27,169	30,190	33,899	35,059	35,843	36,852	34,876	36,350	7.2
Geography									
Boys	12,336	12,891	13,722	14,182	14,502	13,781	13,207	13,157	13,184	−7.0
Girls	8,955	9,295	9,461	10,137	8,350	9,566	9,316	9,453	9,861	−2.7
Total	21,291	22,186	23,183	24,319	22,852	23,347	22,523	22,610	23,045	−5.2
General studies									
Boys	7,753	8,992	10,252	14,867	12,078	12,495	13,659	13,693	14,253	−4.1
Girls	4,089	5,761	6,260	7,444	7,565	7,749	8,966	9,447	10,096	35.6
Total	11,842	14,753	16,512	22,311	19,643	20,244	22,625	23,140	24,349	9.1
Other social science or vocational subjects									
Boys	2,561	3,512	4,028	4,120	4,975	4,727	5,276	5,632	5,284	28.3
Girls	5,616	8,095	8,712	9,462	10,555	10,706	11,620	12,541	13,386	41.5
Total	8,177	11,607	12,740	13,582	15,530	15,433	16,896	18,173	18,670	37.5
All subjects									
Boys	177,604	181,551	186,558	201,390	207,186	208,901	213,139	211,342	217,357	7.9
Girls	123,456	185,457	141,101	147,464	154,137	159,946	164,329	172,748	182,981	24.1
Total	301,060	317,008	327,659	348,854	361,323	368,847	377,468	384,140	400,338	14.8
Total arts	117,893	119,253	121,249	124,620	128,965	126,823	124,275	126,352	130,159	4.4
Total science and technology	115,946	122,040	123,785	130,123	139,274	147,157	154,297	158,989	167,765	28.9
Total social science/vocational	67,221	75,715	82,625	94,111	93,084	94,867	98,896	98,799	102,414	8.8

1 Including all Advanced level mathematical subjects. The figures also include single passes awarded to candidates in mathematics (double subjects).
2 Including English economic history and British constitution.
3 Passes for all years based on the revised subject groupings described in the explanatory notes of 'Statistics of Education, 1976 Volume 2'
Source: HMSO (1983) *DES Statistics of School Leavers 1981*, London, HMSO.

changes which flow from the 'class is the only important political issue' dictum. Of course class *is* important; but so too is gender, and some gender disadvantages, as the discussion of Barrett (1980) in the early part of the chapter suggested, accrue to individuals regardless of their class position. Both class and gender inequalities arise from maldistribution of power as well as resources, and it is this power distribution which must be urgently tackled. There are many developments currently taking place which threaten what few shifts towards greater equality in schools we have already managed to achieve. Expenditure cuts in education on a massive scale mean many schools are struggling to provide the equipment, materials and level of staffing necessary to educate at all; in such a context it is easy to overlook more long-term social goals in favour of short-term economic problems. Developments like TVEI which are trying, hardly for the first time this century (Reeder, 1981), to bring education closer to employment, are likely if they succeed, to impose more fully on schools and colleges the sexual and class divisions of the workplace because in a period of high youth unemployment, the major emphasis is sometimes on 'any job at any pay' rather than on the implications for major social divisions of trying to prod, push and squeeze school leavers into training schemes and jobs. Falling school rolls threaten prospects of gender and class equality, because in secondary schools few LEAs can and do offer adequate curriculum protection as teachers leave or are redeployed elsewhere, and curriculum differentiation is a major source of educational equality. Of course educational change cannot end class or gender divisions, because these are deeply rooted in our society; but it can ameliorate the worst effects of these, and raise awareness of the inequitable nature of those divisions. As the Centre for Contemporary Cultural Studies Education Group wrote in *Unpopular Education* in 1981

> The assertion of the importance and determinancy of gender relations in educational processes has profound implications for educational politics today. It means that older forms of socialist populism which conflated the particular experiences of girls, young women and mothers with those of an undifferentiated ... working class, will no longer suffice as a political starting point ... a new politics of education will have to attend closely to the specific situation of women ... the forms of ... politics that are needed will be both socialist and feminist. (p. 249)

Where Do We Go From Here?

The following would seem to be some of the areas where action ought to be directed if we are to begin to move away from gender-discriminatory forms of education:

1   Reexamine the arguments and evidence in favour of coeducation.

2   Look at the distribution of knowledge and skills in schools between both sexes as well as between pupils of different social class origins.

3   Consider whether the content of what is being taught favours one gender rather than the other.

4   Explore the possibilities of single sex setting (Smith, 1984) for mixed secondary schools where there are gender-related problems about attainment and confidence levels (for example, girls in physical sciences or mathematics).

5   Observe classroom management and other teaching practices for evidence of gender discrimination; if boys are dominant in classrooms (bad for girls and bad for boys too) how can steps be taken to minimize this?

6   Investigate school books, work schemes and work sheets for sexism.

7   Make sure exams and assessment methods aren't gender-biased as well as class-biased. For example Harding (1980) suggests that multiple choice rather than essay-type questions may cause girls to do less well on exams.

8   Analyze the sexual division of labour and power relations between the sexes in schools: the association of particular subjects or areas of responsibility with one sex only; the ways in which teachers relate to and teach pupils of both sexes; the promotion chances of women teachers; the dominance of men in middle and top secondary school management.

9   Monitor the effects of the cuts, and falling rolls on the provision of equal opportunities for both sexes.

10   Search for new ways of organizing comprehensive education so that neither class nor gender divisions reign supreme in the area of the 'hidden curriculum'. Hargreaves (1982) and Shaw (1984) have both claimed that the emphasis in contemporary secondary schools on developing the potential of individual pupils has actually been detrimental because it reduces the

focus on the importance of redressing group inequalities such as class and gender. Hargreaves (1982) argues this case as follows:

> an educational system based on the cultivation of individual pupils will forget that the system will inevitably have social functions and consequences and these cannot be ignored or handed over to others ... Being lost in the culture of individualism, teachers in effect consign the social functions to the hidden curriculum of schooling. (pp. 89–90)

References

ARNOT, M. (1984) 'How shall we educate our sons?' in DEEM, R. (Ed.) *Co-education Reconsidered*, Milton Keynes, Open University Press.

BARRETT, M. (1980) *Women's Oppression Today*, London, Verso Books.

BERLINER, W. (1983) 'Study highlights "O" level pass rate differences', *The Guardian*, 1 July (the NCES study).

BONE, A. (1983) *Girls and Girls Only Schools*, EOC, Manchester.

BREHONY, K. (1984) 'Co-education: perspectives and debates in the early twentieth century' in DEEM, R. (Ed.) *Co-education Reconsidered*, Milton Keynes, Open University Press.

BROWN, R. (1978) 'Work' in ABRAMS, P. (Ed.) *Works, Urbanism and Inequality*, London.

CLARRICOATES, K. (1980) 'The importance of being Ernest ... Emma ... Tom ... Jane: The perception and categorization of gender conformity and gender deviation in primary schools' in DEEM, R. (Ed.) (1980) *Schooling for Women's Work*, London, Routledge and Kegan Paul.

DEEM, R. (1981) 'State policy and ideology in the education of women', *British Journal of Sociology of Education* 2, 2, pp. 131–43.

DEEM, R. (Ed.) (1984) *Co-education Reconsidered*, Milton Keynes, Open University Press.

DEPARTMENT OF EDUCATION AND SCIENCE (1975) 'Curricular differences for boys and girls' *Education Survey 21*, London, HMSO.

DEPARTMENT OF EDUCATION AND SCIENCE (1979) *Aspects of Secondary Education in England* (the Secondary School Survey), London, HMSO.

EDUCATION DIGEST (1983) 'Growing up in Great Britain: The National, Child Development Study', *Education*, 11, November.

GARNSEY, E. (1978) 'Women's work and theories of class stratification', *Sociology*, 12, 2, May, pp. 223–44.

HARDING, J. (1980) 'Sex differences in performance in science examinations' in DEEM, R. (Ed.) *Schooling for Women's* Work, London, Routledge and Kegan Paul.

HARGREAVES, D. (1982) *The Challenge for the Comprehensive School: Culture,*

Curriculum and Community, London, Routledge and Kegan Paul.

ILEA (1982) 'Sex differences and achievement', *ILEA Research and Statistics Report RS 823/82*, London.

LING, V. (1983) 'Education and the labour market for girls in inner London' unpublished M. Phil thesis, London, Polytechnic of the South Bank.

McCABE, T. (1981) 'Girls and leisure' in TOMLINSON, A. (Ed.) *Leisure and Social Control*, Brighton, Brighton Polytechnic.

McROBBIE, A. and McCABE, T. (1981) *Feminism for Girls*, London, Routledge and Kegan Paul.

MARKS, J. and COX, BARONESS (1983) 'NCES: Defence and attack', *Education*, 11, November, pp. 392–3.

MORGAN, D. (1975) 'Women as a social class' in *Social Theory and The Family*, London, Routledge and Kegan Paul.

REEDER, D. (1981) 'A recurring debate: Education and industry' in DALE, R. *et al* (Eds) *Education and the State Volume 1: Schooling and the National Interest*, Lewes, Falmer Press, pp. 177–204.

SHAW, J. (1984) 'The politics of single-sex schools' in DEEM, R. (Ed.) *Co-education Reconsidered,* Milton Keynes, Open University Press.

SMITH, S. (1984) 'Single sex setting' in DEEM, R. (Ed.) *Co-education Reconsidered*, Milton Keynes, Open University Press.

SPENDER, D. (1982) *Invisible Women*, London, Writers and Readers Publishing Cooperative.

STANTONBURY CAMPUS (BRIDGEWATER HALL) SEXISM IN EDUCATION GROUP (1984) 'The realities of mixed schooling' in DEEM, R. (Ed.) *Co-education Reconsidered*, Milton Keynes, Open University Press.

STEVENS, A. (1983) 'Single-sex schools are no better' *The Observer*, 7 August.

WEEKS, A. (1982) 'The Conservative curriculum', *Times Educational Supplement*, 21 May.

WEINBERG, A. (1979) 'An analysis of the persistence of single-sex secondary schools in the English educational system', unpublished Ph.D. thesis, University of Sussex.

WEINBERG, A. (1981) 'Non-decision-making in English education: the case of single-sex secondary schooling' unpublished paper given to the British Sociological Association Conference on 'inequality', University College, Aberystwyth, April.

WESTERGAARD, J. and RESLER, H. (1976) *Class in a Capitalist Society*, Harmondsworth, Penguin.

WILCE, H. (1983) 'Continuing fall in number of women who become heads', *Times Educational Supplement*, 29 July, p. 1.

WILLIS, P. (1977) *Learning to Labour*, Farnborough, Saxon House.

WOLPE, A-M. (1974) 'The official ideology of education for girls' in FLUDE, M. and AHIER, J. (Eds) *Educability, Schools and Society*, London, Croom Helm.

WOLPE, A.-M. (1982) 'Education for what and what education?', *Feminist Review*, 10.

Education and Social Class: Gender: Discussion

Rosemary Deem points out that there is a significant masking of women's socio-economic position because they are automatically given the same status as their husband. If women were assessed on the basis of their own occupation, they would usually be placed in a socio-economic group below that of their husband.

Statistics show that girls achieve better results than boys in GCE 'O' level and CSE exams. But an analysis of the numbers and kinds of subjects studied reveals that girls are offered a far more restricted curriculum than boys. Option choice is a poor name for the narrowing of opportunities which most girls experience after their fourth and fifth year courses. There are fewer training opportunities available for girls and fewer girls than boys go on to higher education.

Despite better overall facilities and a better socializing environment, the move to mixed schools has had some less desirable effects. Boys dominate in the classroom; children are subject to stereotyped peer group pressures; teachers tend to neglect girls, who lack good models with fewer women gaining senior positions and headships. Such factors merely increase the disadvantages for girls.

There seems, however, little support for any move back to single sex schooling or even single sex grouping in mixed schools. But whether to confront those specific problems posed by mixed schools for girls or to adopt a more sensitive and devious approach would depend on each individual school.

In this area of schooling much in secondary education is 'remedial' — putting right what has been mislearnt or ignored at the pre-school and primary stages. It is therefore essential to combat girls' educational disadvantages as early as possible. Primary schools should form links with secondary schools and work towards joint policies for girls' education.

Two particular issues are crucial for all schools: developing a greater level of awareness of equal opportunities by staff, pupils, parents and the local community; and encouraging social education as an integral part of every pupil's curriculum.

1   *Awareness*

Schools should set up working parties on equal opportunities which include representatives of pupils, parents and local primary schools; produce discussion papers with relevant local and national statistics and analyses; invite speakers from outside to act as catalysts for change in school policy with follow-up seminars.

Other techniques include group evaluation; developing proposals for change which can be accepted by the whole staff; putting into practice cross-curricular policies involving staff, pupils, parents the community; effecting relevant changes in school management and the curriculum; and planned reappraisal of what the school is doing.

Schools should assess themselves with the help of the Open University IT Inset programme and the Centre for Evaluation and Development in Teacher Education. The Centre is concerned with observing what actually happens in the classroom, analyzing the learning in progress and judging its value. It aims to link practice with theory.

The practice of continuing and cooperative evaluation encourages appropriate curriculum developments. The Centre supports schools involved in this by providing papers, organizing conferences, visits and meetings as well as offering a consultancy service. In return, schools provide written reports of their class-based studies.

This cooperative approach also includes the initial training of teachers who work alongside their tutors, and teachers from their teaching practice schools. Such an approach can be used to assess current practice in the light of a school's equal opportunities policy and to increase awareness.

2   *Social education*

Social education should aim to instil caring, sensitivity and cooperation as well as initiative, assertiveness and independence. Pupils should be given opportunities to develop self-awareness, including body confidence. Issues such as gender, race and class can be explored through analyzing and understanding the relationships and problems to be found in their own communities.

Valuable tactics include active tutorial methods, some single sex grouping, the introduction of external catalysts, the shock of the unusual, drama and role play, counselling, providing opportunities for pupils to organize their own activities, plus special events, work shadowing and work experience.

A broad social education programme can have many other different and sensitive ways of persuading young people to take advantage of opportunities.

Class of '85

Maurice Plaskow

1985 celebrates the twentieth anniversary of Anthony Crosland's notorious Circular 10/65, which asked local authorities to devize means of ending selection for secondary education at 11 and implementing comprehensive schemes.

1965 was itself twenty years on from the 1944 Education Act, which is still the legislative framework governing education. It set out a blue(sic) print for secondary education for all, looking forward to a compulsory schooling system of at least 5–14, with extensions at both ends, to include nursery and further education for all who wished it.

The Butler Education Act embodied the changing aspirations of a society which had worked gruellingly together for a common aim through six years of war. It was not possible to return to a rigidly divisive structure, with opportunity reserved for a privileged minority. The post-war Labour government began a social reconstruction which attempted to introduce egalitarian principles and end, or at least reduce, the sharply varying provisions within the major areas of community care: health, welfare and education. The 'commanding heights' of the economy were scarcely scaled; rather it was the bleaker valleys where gestures of refertilization were made, and the rundown primary industries of coal, steel and railways were taken out of the hands of private operators who had become caricatures of uncaring, incompetent and inconsiderate employers.

Those old enough to look back and reflect on this forty-year span must find it difficult to assess achievement and disentangle it from frustration and a sense of anger tinged with desperation at the slow speed of change. Cosmetic tinkering is so much easier than radical reconstruction.

The evidence of the papers in this collection, together with the comments, outline the tasks still to be confronted if we are to move nearer to, let alone make a reality of, a democratic, pluralist, egalitarian society.

What is worse, the situation has been compounded and confused because some of the most deeply embedded value-signposts have been uprooted. The places to which they were pointing no longer exist. The concepts of the welfare state, full employment, higher education available to all those wishing to participate, have been peremptorily taken off the agenda.

In the first *Observer* of 1985 (6 January), Dr David Owen wrote:

> There is less unity and more division than for many, many years. Division between the north and south, between the classes, between management and unions, and between the ideologies of left and right.
>
> The millions who are without jobs, and yet who want to contribute to our society, feel alienated and unwanted. Those who work in (or are dependent upon) our public services see falling standards and sense a growing gap between private affluence and public squalor. As the longest national strike in our history grinds on, it is not just the miners who will suffer for years ahead from its consequences.

The divisions over the last few years have become complex and sophisticated. Those of geography, ideology and social class have existed for a long time. The newer, more insidious category is those with jobs and those without.

In the time that it has taken to run (literally) out of steam, cultural attitudes have been turned right around. Arnold of Rugby would have been horrifed at the suggestion that he should be educating his boys for careers in industry or commerce. They would be running their estates, or the Empire. Mass employment was for the masses.

The colonization of the twenty-first century is altogether more subtle. It is of minds, through technology, and the promise of fifth generation, thinking computers ... The creation of artificial intelligence, industrial robots and the consequent imposition of enforced 'leisure' on those who don't want it, by those who haven't got it.

The sequence of expectation — motivation — advancement within which the education system has operated for over 100 years has been shatteringly disrupted. Until the mid-1970s schools could proclaim the catechism that students required a grounding in basic skills on which would be built an academic edifice (of however bizarre design and shaky nature) which would produce qualifications having currency in the marketplace.

The criticism of schools for offering a curriculum which meets neither national nor individual needs predated the alarming rise in unemployment. The orchestration and volume have increased. But the equation between a 'practical' curriculum and economic revival has scarcely been proved: even as a hypothesis the argument is flimsy. And it would sound more convincing if the change to vocational courses aimed at producing wealth were advocated for all, rather than, as one suspects, a desperate attempt to provide activity for the low-motivated, alienated students.

It was the triumph of the thought police of 1984, not conscience, which made cowards of (nearly) all of us, out of fear and self-preservation. Yet there was a dramatic paradox in the mismatch between the rhetoric and the pressures towards normative, compliant behaviour. Power was promised to the people in the name of democratic pluralism. The reality was of punished deviance.

In the tradition of liberal, humane values John Rae, Head of Westminster School, could write in the *New Statesman* (21 September 1973):

> It is not a school's task to produce good citizens any more than it is to produce Christian gentlemen. The school does not give people their political ideals or religious faith, but the means to discover both for themselves. Above all, it gives them the scepticism so that they may leave with the ability to doubt rather than the inclination to believe. In this sense a good schools is subversive of current orthodoxy in politics, religion and learning.

Schools in the late 1980s are facing an impossible task. They have to recognize that for many young people schools represent the most secure, stimulating yet satisfying and enjoyable environment they experience. Students and teachers are aware that the 'real world' (a sad distinction so often made) is increasingly hostile, violent, lacking compassion or generosity of spirit. The media parade the drama of confrontation in their commercial mixtures of fact, fiction and fantasy, so that only the strident hype merits attention.

The folk heroes of 1984 were the bingo millionaires: a new significance for your number coming up. The telling grafitti of our credit card economy was on the walls of Toxteth: 'looting takes the waiting out of wanting'. Deferred gratification is for mugs.

Schools haven't a strong defence against this modern barbarism. 'Education as A Good Thing' sounds feeble against the chart-topping 'I don't want no Educashun.' It's a bit late for ageing prophets to rail against the heresy that education should be useful, and produce economic well-being, as Enoch Powell did (reported in the *Times Educational Supplement*, 4 January 1985):

> Like all things joyous, beautiful and good, education is self-justified ... to claim that we provide public money for teaching and learning in order that our factories and enterprises may be more profitable, productive and competitive is as sinful as to claim that we pay for doctors and hospitals in order to have stronger and healthier soldiers, busier bureaucrats and more productive factory workers. Spending money on education is a work of charity. It consists in giving what is inherently good for the sake of doing good.

There's a nice old-fashioned ring to that. It's also self-deluding, as though the education provided in the public schools were not itself vocational, based on a view of the good and the beautiful being the natural and particular inheritance of their clients, with academic learning as the tools of their acquisition.

The thrust towards a nationally agreed (imposed?) curriculum, within a carefully reconstructed examination framework, will ensure that subversion will require even greater energy and cunning to survive. The well-intentioned disingenuousness of 'education for capability' allows the infiltration of training for technicians under the rubric of practical knowledge. While the academic diet of the increasingly squeezed proportion of the elite remains protected and inviolate. The meek will inherit the earth all right — to dig, burrow and finally lie in.

The central issues are essentially those of attitudes and values. *Comprehensive* is all-inclusive, or it is a sham. Our education system is remarkable in that it is largely controlled by people (mainly men) who have not themselves been through the maintained sector, nor do they entrust their own children to it.

This must mean that those who support and use private schools, or indeed the private health service, believe that they are buying superior quality and privilege. Arguments on the basis of 'freedom', allowing people to spend their money however they wish, simply will not do. We do not allow people to indulge their whims, desires and selfishness indiscriminately if their actions are likely to damage others. A strong, influential private sector draws talented teachers trained at public expense, and many talented students, away from our public institutions. To this extent these are impoverished and handicapped, not least because the parents are those who could be expected to campaign most vigorously for quality and resources, if their own children were in ordinary schools.

It is surely untenable to talk glibly in terms of one nation in these circumstances. The hypocrisy is further compounded as long as higher education remains the preserve of the more privileged within society, supplying overwhelmingly those who achieve positions of power and influence.

The maintained schools are subject to harsh financial constraints which have resulted in a fall of some 2 per cent of public spending on education in recent years — from nearly 12 per cent to under 10 per cent. Independent schools simply raise their fees, or send appeals to their Gucci-shod alumni.

The divisions which we can now chart affect not just life-styles, but life-chances and self-esteem. Employment prospects in the north and south are dramatically different. A growing helplessness affects aspirations, motivation and thereby levels of achievement. Young people see little point in struggling for five academic 'O' levels whose market value has gone the way of the rest of our currency.

It is not surprising that initiatives like the Technical and Vocational Education Initiative (TVEI) and the Certificate of Pre-Vocational Education (CPVE) look more attractive to those desperately seeking courses which seem to have some relevance to employment and self-development.

It is ironic (it was at the time, too) that Sir Keith Joseph asked the Sheffield North of England Conference in 1984 whether we were at a watershed. The water has been gathering speed fast, and is likely to engulf us in a flood, both economically and socially.

There are perverse forces impeding reconciliation. Paradoxically, the efforts to achieve a common curriculum with greater accountability within a single assessment system, could make the most significant contribution since 1944 to the realization of a comprehensive framework. But not if, at the same time, training is separated from education in both responsibility and practice. Differential outcomes would become even more firmly embedded, and values of fierce individual competitiveness rule instead of constructive cooperation and concern for the whole community.

In his important book on the challenge to comprehensives, David Hargreaves urged that schools should become more community orientated. He posed the stark polarization between the traditional public/ grammar school objective of the individualist scholar, against the new model of the well-indoctrinated, utilitarian citizen. The balance needs to rest on a curriculum which imaginatively combines an introduction to knowledge, skills and understandings, practical capability, expressive and aesthetic development and engagement in community activity. It is difficult to see any other way forward which would harness the energy of the young to useful tasks which could provide satisfaction and worthwhileness when traditional work might not be regularly available.

The first necessary condition is for people to feel that progress is possible towards personal fulfilment in a convivial community.

As the earlier chapter on curriculum indicates, the language of educational discourse has significantly changed. The vocabulary now includes concepts of consultation and negotiation, participation and evaluation. These positive values could transform the educational enterprise, and in their turn affect the wider ethos in society. Not as sensational a scenario as *1984*, but infinitely more agreeable a prospect for the new millenium.

Notes on Contributors

Peter Mortimore taught in London, and has been Director of Research and Statistics, ILEA, since 1978. He is visiting Professor of Education at the London Institute, 1985/86.

Malcolm Skilbeck was Professor of Curriculum Studies, London Institute of Education. He has returned to Australia as Vice-Chancellor, Monash University.

John Gray is a Reader in Education, Sheffield University, and director of the ESRC-funded Contexts Project.

Ben Jones is a research fellow, Sheffield University.

David Jesson is a lecturer in education, Sheffield University.

Richard Pring is a Professor of Education, Exeter University.

Stephen Ball is a lecturer in the sociology of education, King's College, London. He is author of *Beachside Comprehensive*, and of *Comprehensive Schooling: a Reader*.

Alan Little is Lewisham Professor of Social Administration, Goldsmiths' College, and author of *Studies in the Multicultural Curriculum* (Schools Council), and many other publications on race.

Harold Rosen was a Professor of Education, London Institute of Education, and author of many publications on language.

Sue Holmes was director of the Schools Council Industry Project (SCIP). She is now an Inspector with the London Borough of Merton.

Ian Jamieson was Research Director, Schools Council Industry Project. He is now lecturer in Education, University of Bath.

Rosemary Deem is a lecturer in the School of Education, Open University. She is also a Buckinghamshire County Councillor.

Maurice Plaskow is an educational consultant, having been a Curriculum Officer with the Schools Council, 1970–84.

Caerleon
Library